Praise for

THE WEISER CONCISE GUIDE TO
ALEISTER CROWLEY

"Dr. Kaczynski's contribution to the canon of beginner's guides to Thelema and Magick stands apart from its predecessors in that it sets forth a simple yet comprehensive map to the Crowley universe. This book will be valuable not only to those who are looking for a reliable introduction to Crowley's life and work, but also to practicing Thelemites as a new tool in their efforts to bring the Law of Light, Life, Love and Liberty to Humanity."

— Sabazius X°, National Grand Master General,
U.S. Grand Lodge of Ordo Templi Orientis

"Trying to capture the essence of the life, literature, and wisdom of a man so prolific, complex, and masterful as Aleister Crowley is a daunting task. To encapsulate it into a basic primer is even more challenging. Richard Kaczynski has succeeded admirably, and in so doing, has given a valuable introduction to Crowley, the esoteric Orders of the A∴A∴ and O.T.O., and their respective teachings. An excellent answer to the question, 'Where do I begin?'"

— J. Daniel Gunther,
author of *Initiation in the Aeon of the Child*

"Like the complex and monumental scenario of a Wagnerian opera, the life and works of Aleister Crowley stand as an epic tale of gods, magick, adventure, and romance. With this Concise Guide, Dr. Kaczynski offers us for the first time a truly proper 'overture' to this amazing and important spiritual figure—a Crowley digest that is delightfully digestible."

— Lon Milo DuQuette,
author of *The Magick of Aleister Crowley*

THE WEISER CONCISE GUIDE SERIES

ALEISTER CROWLEY

RICHARD KACZYNSKI, PH.D.

EDITED AND INTRODUCED BY
JAMES WASSERMAN

WEISERBOOKS
San Francisco, CA / Newburyport, MA

First published in 2009 by
Red Wheel/Weiser, LLC
With offices at:
500 Third Street, Suite 230
San Francisco, CA 94107
www.redwheelweiser.com

ISBN: 978-1-57863-456-9

Library of Congress Cataloging-in-Publication Data
available upon request.

Cover design by Maija Tollefson
Text design by Studio 31
Typeset in Adobe Sabon

Cover photo of Aleister Crowley on the Deosai Plateau in the
Himalayas during the Kachenjunga expedition of 1905.
Reproduced from *The Book of Lies* by permission of
Ordo Templi Orientis, with thanks to James Strain.

Printed in Canada
TCP
10 9 8 7 6 5 4 3 2 1

CONTENTS

ACKNOWLEDGMENTS

CROWLEY OFTEN SAID that for an idea to be true, it must contain its own contradiction. Thus a concise guide to his work is arguably an impossibility. What one person concludes is crucial to an understanding of his magical system, another may reject as superfluous. With that said, several people reviewed this manuscript who have our deepest respect and gratitude. In thanking them for their assistance, we also absolve them of any responsibility for our choices. In alphabetical order, Hymenaeus Beta, J. Daniel Gunther, Stephen J. King, J. P. Lund, and David Scriven all provided expert guidance and invaluable (sometimes stinging) criticism. Daniel Pineda made several excellent editorial suggestions. Keith Stump offered encouragement and proofreading. Thanks to James Strain for providing the cover image many years ago, to Anthony W. Iannotti for the *Diary of a Drug Fiend* cover scan, and to Kent Finne, Stella Grey, and Nancy Wasserman for reviewing the manuscript. Finally, we are grateful to Ordo Templi Orientis for allowing us permission to quote Crowley's works and access images from their collection; and the Warburg Institute of the University of London, the Beinecke Rare Book and Manuscript Library of Yale University, and the New York Public Library for access to their manuscript materials on Aleister Crowley, Mary Butts, and W. B. Yeats, respectively.

Richard Kaczynski and James Wasserman

JAMES WASSERMAN

Do what thou wilt shall be the whole of the Law.

I HAD ORIGINALLY INTENDED to write this book myself. Time constraints suggested I offer it to someone I could respect and trust. Richard Kaczynski was the natural choice. A gifted scholar, he is well-versed in Thelema (the Greek word meaning "will," by which Crowley's teaching is designated). Richard is the author of the excellent biography of Aleister Crowley, *Perdurabo*. He is a high-ranking member of O.T.O. whose service has gained him the admiration and appreciation of many. Our friendship allowed me to speak directly about my concerns for a doctrinally accurate book. He cheerfully and humbly accepted my condition that the work be vetted and approved by a carefully chosen board of Thelemic scholars and magicians.

I am happy the gods have directed the project as they have. Richard and I come from different generations. He will be closer to the shared experiences of many readers than I might be. In 1977, the year he was enthusiastically bicycling home at age 14 with his first copy of *Magick in Theory and Practice* tucked in his backpack, I was 29 and in the throes of a magical ordeal demanding I develop "certainty, not faith" to sustain my very life and sanity.

This book is not an attempt to provide a broad survey of current Thelemic "offerings," e.g. the multiplicity of recent "orders" and "schools of interpretation." We acknowledge one A∴A∴ and one O.T.O.

We will also avoid the interpretations so common to much post-Crowley magical literature. This is an attempt to document Crowley's teaching as he designed his system, with some reference to the modern development of Thelema. O.T.O. Frater Superior Hymenaeus Beta has spent many years brilliantly editing the corpus of Crowley literature. I also highly recommend J. Daniel Gunther's *Initiation in the Aeon of the Child: The Inward Journey* (Ibis Press, 2009), which is, in my opinion, the most important doctrinal contribution since Crowley's death.

Otherwise, my recommendations on magical literature have remained unchanged for decades. Read Crowley. If you don't understand what he is saying, buy a dictionary. If you're still unclear about what he means, keep trying. Once in a while you may be lucky enough to meet someone who can help shed light on the subject. I sincerely hope Richard Kaczynski and this book can serve that function for you. Crowley gave us a very intelligible guide to the importance he placed on his individual writings by organizing them in a literary classification system. Richard explains this fully on page 33. Such a system is unique in the annals of religious history and is further confirmation of Aleister Crowley's stature as a world teacher.

On a personal level, this book conjures the spirits of departed loved ones and guides—angel-headed hipsters whose lives are intimately entwined with my earlier years and quest for an understanding of Aleister Crowley—Grady McMurtry, Harry Smith, Angus Maclise, and Richard Gernon.

May this book serve as a Lamp to illumine your steps as you seek to discover your True Will.

Love is the law, love under will.

DISCLAIMER

WHEN A PERSON begins to study Aleister Crowley, he or she enters a UNIVERSE rather than a "field of study." It is impossible for any individual to capture his essence. Like the parable about the blind men describing an elephant, one can only report what one is able to perceive. Add to that the limited amount of space available in an introductory book of this nature, and the reader will understand that we are only able to offer a glimpse of Crowley's teachings.

Three Quick Tips on Thelemic Etiquette

1. Please be sure to properly capitalize "Do what thou wilt shall be the whole of the Law," or "Love is the law, love under will" in your correspondence. All quotes from a Class A text should be spelled and capitalized verbatim, "Change not as much as the style of a letter ..." (AL I:54).

2. The name "Crowley" rhymes with "holy." He gave the definitive clue in his satirical poem "The Convert," first published in *The Winged Beetle*.

   "Where are you going, so meek and holy?"
   "I'm going to temple to worship Crowley."

3. We avoid the modern spelling of "magickal" for "magical," or "magickian" for "magician." There is not a single example of A.C. using that orthography in a bookcase full of his books. He coined the word "magick" to define his system, spelled the adjective "magical," and called its practitioners "magicians."

Overview

I STILL REMEMBER reading my first Crowley book, *Magick in Theory and Practice*, at the tender and impressionable age of 14. It came highly recommended by the proprietor of the local occult bookstore, who had taken me under his wing. Rushing home on my bicycle and cracking open that sleek, black-covered Dover paperback, I prepared myself to behold the great Mysteries—with a capital, flashing, neon M. And so I read those famous early words:

> Witness mine hand:
>
> TO ΜΕΓΑ ΘΗΡΙΟΝ (תריון): The Beast 666; MAGUS 9°=2□ A∴A∴ who is The Word of the Aeon THELEMA; whose name is called V.V.V.V.V. 8°=3□ A∴A∴ in the City of the Pyramids; OU MH 7°=4□; OL SONUF VAORESAGI 6°=5□, and ... ... 5°=6□ A∴A∴ in the Mountain of Abiegnus: but FRATER PERDURABO in the Outer Order or the A∴A∴ and in the World of men upon the Earth, Aleister Crowley of Trinity College, Cambridge.

I didn't understand a single word of it. Clearly it meant *something*, but the meaning played a sadistic hide-and-seek game with my consciousness, like one of those fantastic dreams that becomes less coherent the more you awaken. I vowed to decipher this book. This has turned into a lifetime task. There were no beginner's guides. I hope this *Concise Guide to Aleister Crowley* will help the reader gain a more clear sense of his system.

Crowley had an imposing reputation in life, and since death he casts an even larger shadow. He left his mark in so many different ways that he defies categorization. Most of us would be satisfied to accomplish just one of his many impressive achievements:

- A practicing occultist whose mastery of Western magick and Eastern mysticism was unsurpassed by any of his contemporaries, and who continues to be an icon for many of today's practicing magicians.
- The founder and prophet of the new religious movement of Thelema, best known by its oft-misunderstood catchphrase, "Do what thou wilt shall be the whole of the Law."

- A prolific poet whose *Collected Works*, by age thirty, filled three volumes, and whose last published work, *Olla*, was subtitled *Sixty Years of Song*.
- A maverick mountaineer whose numerous innovations and world records in the sport are acknowledged by even his most vocal critics.
- An adventurer whose exploits in the Far East were serialized by *Vanity Fair* magazine as "A Burmese River."
- An impresario who took the violin troupe the Ragged Ragtime Girls on a tour of St. Petersburg, Russia.
- A British secret agent who marshaled his literary and occult connections to the service of his country, including (reputedly) the invention of the "V for Victory" sign as a magical antidote to the swastika.
- A ranked chess master who could trounce many players without even looking at the chess board.
- A pioneering entheogenic explorer who conducted psychedelic experiments with mescaline.
- Producer and star of *The Rites of Eleusis*, a series of ritualistic plays featuring an innovative blend of magick, drama, music, and poetry.
- One of the most unjustly vilified men in the history of journalism, garnering headlines like "The Wickedest Man in the World" and "A Man We'd Like To Hang."

More mistruth and rumor has circulated about Aleister Crowley than perhaps any other figure in recent history. When the reporter Henry Hall introduced him to readers of the *New York World Sunday Magazine*, he wrote, "Some said that he was a man of real attainments, others that he was a faker. All agreed that he was extraordinary."[1] Crowley openly defied social conventions, challenging people to examine what they really believed and why they believed it. He confronted blind faith with rational skepticism. Yet he likewise challenged the skeptic with scientific illuminism, a systematic approach to spirituality that he described as "The method of science, the aim of religion."[2]

---

1 Hall, Henry N. "Master Magician Reveals Weird Supernatural Rites." *The World Magazine*, 13 December 1914, p. 9, 17.
2 This was the motto of his journal *The Equinox*, published between 1909 and 1913.

Crowley was extremely well-read and often assumed the same of his readers, so his technical works are often difficult to understand—and easy to *mis*understand. This makes him a challenging figure to approach as a reader—or, for that matter, as a writer.

These pages offer an overview of Aleister Crowley's life and magick—an introduction for newcomers, and a refresher for old hands. Magick and mysticism are the focus. However, since these are often inseparable from his poetry and other activities, the discussion will be broader. The first chapter presents a portrait of Aleister Crowley. Part I offers a look at the magical and mystical societies he championed, namely A∴A∴ (the Order of the Star called S.S.), Ordo Templi Orientis (O.T.O., or Order of Oriental Templars), and Ecclesia Gnostica Catholica (E.G.C. or Gnostic Catholic Church). Part II offers a practical approach to a number of Crowley's occult practices. The appendices provide several core documents of Thelema and contact information. The chapters are designed to be read in whatever order interests you most; read it cover to cover, or, if you prefer, skip to the practical material and read the background information later.

In order to get the most out of studying this book, you will need to get up and *do* the practical instructions in Part II. Magick cannot be understood by simply reading about it. The truth is that these meditations, exercises and practices *do* produce altered states of consciousness—ways of thinking, seeing, and experiencing the world that are different from your ordinary consciousness. If you don't try these things, you'll never "get" it. We have presented the ritual instructions in Crowley's own words to avoid either interpretation or error. Try it, and you'll experience for yourself that *magick works*.

Set aside your preconceptions and dismiss the rumors. Crowley was certainly a complex, controversial, and colorful man, but the truth is far more interesting than the legend.

CHAPTER ONE

A LIFE OF ALEISTER CROWLEY

ALEISTER CROWLEY was born on October 12, 1875, as Edward Alexander Crowley. He was named after his father, Edward Crowley (1834–1887), who had been named after his father before him (ca. 1796–1856). Although Edward the Third would change his name to Aleister (a Gaelic form of his middle name, Alexander) upon entering the University of Cambridge, the forces that shaped Aleister Crowley into the magician, prophet, and rebel *To Mega Therion* were very much in place from birth.

In his *Confessions*, Crowley made several dubious claims for predestined greatness: He was of noble descent (from "the Breton family of de Quérouaille—which gave England a Duchess of Portsmouth"[1]). He was born with the characteristic marks of a Buddha (having four hairs on his chest in the form of a swastika, and being tongue-tied, requiring childhood surgery to cut the fræ-num under his tongue to allow him to speak). And his birthplace of Leamington was in the same county (Warwicksire) as England's *other* great poet, William Shakespeare.

The Crowley Family

The Crowleys were a Quaker family from Alton that had run a brewery near Croydon, Surrey, for over two hundred years. In 1821, Aleister's great-uncle, Abraham Crowley (ca. 1796–1864), and his sons Charles Sedgefield and Henry, purchased the Brew-house in Turk Street from James Baverstock, who had introduced scientific instrumentation into brewing. A.C.S. & H. Crowley—later Crowley & Co.—was hugely successful in offering beer and a sandwich for four pence at its Alton Alehouses, essentially invent-ing the pub lunch. The success of the business left an impression in the literature of the era: In *Edmund Yates: His Recollections and Experiences* (1884), Yates recounts lunching at "Crowley's Alton Alehouse," whose shops were "exceedingly popular with young men who did not particularly care about hanging round the bars

---

1 Crowley, Aleister. *The Confessions of Aleister Crowley*. Abridged edi-tion, John Symonds and Kenneth Grant, eds. London: Jonathan Cape, 1969, p. 35.

A label from one of Crowley's Alton Ales

or taverns" (vol. 1, p. 121). *In Praise of Ale* (1888) describes how the firm "L. and S.W.R. transports 'Alton Ale' in large quantities to London" (p. 462). Even Charles Dickens, in the November 11, 1854, edition of his weekly journal *Household Words*, remarked that Alton's growth boom included "a feeding place, 'established to supply the Railway public with a first-rate sandwich and a sparkling glass of Crowley's Ale...'" (p. 291).

The Crowley family also prospered through involvement in the British rail by the brothers Charles Sedgefield and Edward. Charles Sedgefield was director of several railways—including the London and Croydon Railway and the Sudbury and Halstead Railway—and deputy chairman of the Direct London and Portsmouth Railway Company. Aleister's grandfather Edward similarly directed the London, Brighton, and South Coast Railway, plus the Direct London and Portsmouth Railway Company and the Brighton and Chichester Railway.[2] In November, 1852—following a tragic

---

2 Tuck, Henry, *Railway Directory for 1845: Containing the Names of the Directors and Principal Officers of the Railways in Great Britain*, London: Railway Times Office, 1845; Glynn, Henry, *Reference Book to the Incorporated Railway Companies of England and Wales*, London: John Weale,

collision in Red Hill on the Brighton Line managed by his father—Jonathan Sparrow Crowley invented "Crowley's Safety Switch and Self-Acting Railway Signals" to prevent such tragedies in the future.[3] Aleister Crowley alluded to this family history when he quipped, "My father would refuse to buy railway shares because railways were not mentioned in the Bible!"[4]

On March 24, 1877—seven months before Aleister's second birthday—the Crowleys sold their brewery to Abraham Crowley's son-in-law, Joseph Burrell. Edward Crowley II shrewdly reinvested his money into Amsterdam's waterworks. While the investment details are unknown, English businessmen around this time founded the highly successful Amsterdam Water Works Company in 1865, whose 1872 expansion drew thousands of workers to the company. It is likely that Edward Crowley invested money into this very business. According to A.C., his father quipped sardonically that "he had been an abstainer for nineteen years, during which he had shares in a brewery. He had now ceased to abstain for some time, but all his money was invested in a waterworks."[5] The family's prosperity is demonstrated by the fact that, in their household in Warwickshire, the servants outnumbered family members.

Edward Crowley broke from his family's Quaker roots, embracing a fledgling fundamentalist faith known as the Brethren (or Plymouth Brethren). The faith was based on Matthew 18:20 ("Where two or three are gathered together in my name, there am I in the midst of them"), arguing radically that believers require no priests or ministers to celebrate the Lord's Supper. The faith interpreted the Bible literally, with the precise date of creation ascertainable to roughly 4000 B.C.E. Christ's return was also believed to be imminent, and some even regarded financial investments and savings as evidence of lack of faith. Edward Crowley was an active and prolific spokesperson for the Brethren faith. Naylor (2004) lists over one hundred different tracts that Edward Crowley printed for distribution both by mail and on his walking tours around England.

1847; Charles Barker & Sons, *The Joint Stock Companies' Directory for 1876*, London: John King & Co., 1867.

3 Dickens, Charles, "Self-Acting Railway Signals," *Household* Words 1853, 7(155):43–5; Anonymous, "Crowley's Safety Switch and Self-Acting Railway Signals," *The Mechanics' Magazine* 1853, 58(1537):66–7.

4 Crowley, *The World's Tragedy*, p. xiii.

5 *Confessions*, p. 46.

He was important enough to earn a mention in *The History of the Brethren 1826–1936*.

The Brethren faith was indeed Spartan: They did not celebrate traditional Christian holidays, believing them (rightly) to be based on older pagan festivals. Childhood reading was strictly monitored and restricted to approved books, of which the Bible was most encouraged for continual study. Young Aleister was only allowed to play with other Brethren children. And when he misbehaved, his mother said he was the Beast from Revelation—a moniker that would, in later years, wind up sticking. Nevertheless, Crowley reports a happy early childhood during which he clearly idolized his charismatic and deeply religious father.

Events in his early teen years, however, embittered him against religion. It began with the frequent schisms (or "divisions") that plagued the Brethren. Young Crowley couldn't grasp how one day dear family friends were numbered among the chosen and righteous ones to enter God's kingdom, and then the next day were condemned sinners with whom he was forbidden contact. When his preaching father developed tongue cancer, the irony could not have been lost on young Crowley. Upon the advice of the church, Edward Crowley shunned conventional medicine in favor of homeopathic treatment, moving the family homestead to Southampton in order to be closer to his doctor. He died within a year. Aleister was some six months shy of his twelfth birthday.

So beloved was the memory of his father that Crowley would not tolerate anyone's encroachment on his domain. When his mother took up Edward Crowley's mailing list and continued to send out Brethren literature, A.C. characterized her as "a brainless bigot of the most narrow, illogical and inhuman type."[6] And when they moved in with his uncle, Tom Bond Bishop, himself a lay preacher and philanthropist, Crowley regarded his faith as "extraordinarily narrow, ignorant and bigoted Evangelicalism."[7] He resented his uncle so much that he dedicated his parody of fundamentalism, "Elder Eel," to him.

The exclusive schools he attended meted out injustice from bullies and staff alike. When students became ill after a well-intentioned program to feed the homeless, it was considered God's punishment for some undisclosed sin. Crowley became rebellious

6 *Confessions*, p. 36.
7 *Confessions*, p. 54.

after his father's death, which his masters, at first, attributed to grief. But when Crowley was anonymously accused of an unspecified immorality, he was isolated from his fellow students outside class time and fed only bread and water until he confessed. He had no idea what he supposedly did, and came down with a life-threatening kidney disease (albuminuria) before his mother and uncle un-enrolled him, and sent him for a cure of country air and exercise with a private tutor. Fortunately, his tutor was more liberal, and demonstrated to the recovering Crowley that one could be a good person yet still enjoy tobacco, alcohol, and sex. "He taught me sense and manhood," Crowley recalled, "and I shall not easily forget my debt to him."[8]

Although embittered by his experience of the Brethren faith, Crowley did not reject religion outright. "I did not hate God or Christ, but merely the God and Christ of the people whom I hated."[9] In his early college years, an existential crisis led him to the realization that all ambitions and careers are ultimately lost in the sands of time. He concluded the only thing that mattered, that endured, was the spirit. His quest for spiritual truth led him to mysticism and occultism and the search for the Great White Lodge, an invisible college of enlightened teachers offering guidance to those determined enough to find its door. So the stage was set for this sheltered, spiritual, wealthy, handsome, and profoundly rebellious young man to become Aleister Crowley.

College

Entering Cambridge's Trinity College in the fall of 1895 in moral sciences, he enjoyed his majority and independence like any other college student: with experimentation. He voraciously read the books once forbidden to him and quickly amassed a large library of poetry, religion, history, philosophy, and science. Inspired by the likes of Shelley, Keats, Browning, and Swinburne, he began to write his own poetry, alternately florid, sensuous, and sarcastic. He moved in Aesthetic or Decadent circles, befriending Oscar Wilde's publisher Leonard Smithers, who helped him to self-publish his poetry. He experimented with sex, complaining famously of "the stupidity of having had to waste uncounted priceless hours

8 *The World's Tragedy*, p. xx.
9 *Confessions*, p. 73.

in chasing what ought to have been brought to the back door every evening with the milk!"[10]; he even lived for a time as the "wife" of the Cambridge transvestite performer Herbert Charles Jerome Pollitt (a.k.a. Diane de Rougy [1871–1942]). At this time, he also dropped the names "Alick" and "Alec" of his boyhood, adopting instead a Gaelic form, Aleister.

Although he competed in the Cambridge chess club and Magpie and Stump Debating Society, he was more of a loner at heart. He did not attend chapel, which was mandatory for students (he claimed it was against the faith in which he was raised). Nor did he take meals with his classmates, paying the kitchen staff to bring meals to his room at times that better suited him. And he often missed classes, with one professor even permitting the precocious scholar to skip lectures and study independently. After three years of college, he, "like Byron, Shelley, Swinburne and Tennyson,"[11] left without graduating.

Poetry

In his lifetime, Aleister Crowley published scores of books, pamphlets, broadsheets, and articles, a vast portion of them being poetic works. His poetry has always garnered mixed reviews. The *Athenæum*, for instance, disliked his poetry's sensuality.[12] Others, most notably G.K. Chesterton (1874–1936), derided its subject matter. W.B. Yeats notably said that Crowley "has written about six lines, amid much bad rhetoric, of real poetry."[13] For all his critics, however, Crowley also has his fans. Significantly, *English Review* editor Austin Harrison called Crowley the greatest metrical poet since Swinburne. J.F.C. Fuller, fifty years after parting ways with Crowley, still regarded him as "one of England's greatest lyric poets, and among those of France, comparable with Rimbaud and Baudelaire," and certain of his works as "of the highest poetic genius."[14] Perhaps the highest tribute possible is his inclusion in

10 *Confessions*, p. 113.

11 *Confessions*, p. 166.

12 Stephensen, *The Legend of Aleister Crowley*, p. 37.

13 W.B. Yeats to John Quinn, 21 March 1915, John Quinn Memorial Collection, New York Public Library.

14 Fuller, J.F.C. "Aleister Crowley 1898-1911: An Introductory Essay." In Keith Hogg, *666: Bibliotheca Crowleyana: Catalogue of a Unique*

The Cambridge Poets 1900–1913 (1913) and The Oxford Book of English Mystical Verse (1916). As Amphlett Micklewright wrote in his appreciation of Crowley,

> It is not always the case that the poems of occultists are essential to an understanding of their work. But Aleister Crowley is fundamentally an artist. He is a creative personality, expressing his individuality in terms of rhythm. His sense of the rhythmic, which ultimately implies the sense of a fundamental beauty, is aptly expressed whether in prose or in verse; his art is a necessary entrance to an understanding of his occultism.[15]

Enter the Golden Dawn

During his recovery from albuminuria, Crowley discovered a love—and talent—for mountain climbing; indeed, he set records around the world and helped to introduce innovations into the sport. While vacationing in the Swiss Alps in 1898, he stopped in a beer hall and wound up giving an impromptu lecture on alchemy. He was mortified when, afterwards, one of the drinkers introduced himself as Julian L. Baker, an analytical chemist and alchemist. He promised to introduce Crowley to an invisible college once they returned to London.

That invisible college wound up being the Order of the Golden Dawn (G.D.), the most celebrated and influential late nineteenth-century magical society. Founded in 1888 as an outgrowth of the Societas Rosicruciana in Anglia (S.R.I.A.), it disseminated occult teachings without the S.R.I.A.'s requirements of belief in the Christian Trinity, being a Master Mason, and being male. Its founding members—William Wynn Westcott (1848–1925), William Robert Woodman (1828–1891), and Samuel Liddell MacGregor Mathers (1854–1918)—were all accomplished in esoteric freemasonry, Rosicrucianism, and occult studies. Much of the group's ritual and study material drew on their published and unpublished writings.

Collection of Books, Pamphlets, Proof Copies, MSS., etc., by, about, or connected with Aleister Crowley: Formed, and with an Introductory Essay, by Major-General J.F.C. Fuller, Tenterden, Kent, 1966, p. 8.

15 Amphlett Micklewright, F. H. "Aleister Crowley, Poet and Occultist." The Occult Review 1945, 72(2):41–6.

The group began to founder after Woodman died in 1891. Westcott succeeded Woodman as head of the S.R.I.A., unofficially leaving stewardship of the Golden Dawn to Mathers, whose recent move to Paris would later leave London members weary of answering to an absentee hierophant.

Crowley joined the G.D. in November 1898. He mastered all the material—even gaining a private tutor in Allan Bennett, the Order's most respected magician—and advanced steadily through the five "Outer Order" grades. Ironically, Crowley's friendship with the G.D.'s leader Mathers hindered his advancement into the higher degrees, as the senior London members united almost unanimously in opposition to Crowley's further advancement. Just as he hit this glass ceiling, Mathers issued an ultimatum to the London lodge: either sign an oath of obedience to him or face expulsion. A predictable schism ensued. Disappointed that the order didn't live up to the lofty ideal of the Great White Lodge, Crowley drifted away from the G.D. and concluded that Mathers was no longer in contact with the Secret Chiefs who ran the invisible college. Mathers would ultimately expel Crowley some years later.

For much of the next four years, he traveled the world. He set mountaineering records in Mexico and the Himalayas. He went big game hunting in India and Sri Lanka. He lived in Sri Lanka with Allan Bennett, studying yoga, Hinduism, and Buddhism. He was part of the circle of artists, poets, and writers at Le Chat Blanc in Paris, where he mixed with W. Somerset Maugham, Rodin, and, most importantly, his future brother-in-law, portrait painter Gerald Kelly.[16]

The Book of the Law

Crowley first met Gerald Kelly when both were Cambridge undergraduates. Through him, in 1903, he also met Gerald's sister, Rose.

---

16 Before achieving fame as the author of *Of Human Bondage* (1915), William Somerset Maugham (1874–1965) modeled the title character of *The Magician* (1908) after Crowley. French artist Auguste Rodin (1840–1917) befriended Crowley for defending his sculpture of Balzac, and they collaborated on *Seven Lithographs By Clot from the Water-Colours of Auguste Rodin with a Chaplet of Verse By Aleister Crowley* (1907). Gerald Festus Kelly (1879–1972) was studying under Canadian impressionist James Wilson Morrice during this period; he would go on to be knighted in 1945 and to serve as president of the Royal Academy from 1949 to 1954.

The Stele of Revealing, obverse   The Stele of Revealing, reverse

She confided in Crowley an unhappy circumstance. Under pressure from her family, she was awaiting the arrival of a suitor from America, but was actually in love with a married man with whom she was having an affair. Crowley chivalrously offered to get her off the hook by marrying her and letting her conduct her affairs with whomever she pleased. Rose agreed, and they slipped away and eloped early the next morning, much to the family's surprise and dismay.

To their own surprise, the newlyweds found themselves in love. Crowley took Rose on a honeymoon to Egypt, where he showed her the pyramids and demonstrated some magick in the King's Chamber. She responded by later going into a dreamy state and speaking distractedly about how the Egyptian god Horus wanted a word with Crowley. Although he didn't take it seriously at first, he ultimately quizzed Rose—or whoever was speaking through her—about Horus. Remarkably, Rose, who knew nothing at all about Egyptian mythology, answered every question perfectly. As a final test, Crowley took her to a museum and asked her to point out an image of Horus. Walking past several other images of the god, Rose pointed to a wooden stele across the room. Not only did the stele show a picture of Horus, but it bore museum catalog number 666. It was all the proof he needed.

Rose described a ceremony (later called the Supreme Ritual) for Crowley to perform on March 20, 1904, the vernal equinox. He was subsequently instructed to go into his Cairo flat at precisely noon on April 8, 9, and 10 and, for the next hour, write down the words he heard. This he did, and the result is *The Book of the Law*.[17] It is a text that exhilarated, bewildered, and even shocked him. It not only declares the beginning of a new era for humanity, but names Crowley its prophet as the Beast 666.[18] It spells out a doctrine of joy, empowerment, and individual liberty, and calls on all people to discover and fulfill their true nature. Its central tenet is "Do what thou wilt shall be the whole of the Law." Crowley would ultimately devote his life to spreading its word.

At first, however, he didn't know what to make of *The Book of the Law*. He sent typescripts to some colleagues who were just as nonplussed as he was. So he set it aside and returned to his other pursuits.

Mountain Climbing

When Aleister Crowley set out in 1905 to be the first person to climb Kangchenjunga—the third highest mountain in the world— he'd already amassed impressive credentials in the sport, which he took up at age 17. According to mountaineering writer Colin Wells:

> Even without his diabolical extracurricular activities, Crowley's climbing legacy ensures him a place in mountaineering's Hall of Fame. For a time, he held claim to the world altitude record and the hardest free moves done on rock. Though his stint on the heights was comparatively short-lived ... he was part of the leading pack of early rock climbers who created a recognizably modern style of technical climbing in the English

---

17 Technically called *Liber AL vel Legis*.

18 *The Sword of Song* (1904) reveals that Crowley had begun identifying himself with 666 before receiving *The Book of the Law*. Magically speaking, there is nothing evil about the numeral 666. It actually symbolizes the Sun; because its traditional number is 6, so are its extensions 6x6 (or 36) and $\Sigma(1\text{-}36)$ or $1+2+3+...+36 = 666$.

Lake District. He was also the first to dare climb the uniquely insecure chalk cliffs of England's south coast.

In mountaineering, he was the first to seriously attempt K2 and Kangchenjunga, and pioneered guideless climbing in the Alps.[19]

He'd previously (1902) been on the team that tackled K2, the second-highest mountain in the world. The only thing keeping him from the world's highest peak, Mt. Everest, was that Europeans were not allowed access at the time. The Kangchenjunga climb was Crowley's first time leading an expedition, and his style—mixing authoritarianism with daring that often bordered on folly—did not sit well with his team. They quarreled over what was the best ascent up the mountain (history ultimately proved Crowley to be correct). At one point part of his team mutinied and left the expedition; during their descent, Swiss climber Alexis Pache and several porters were killed in an avalanche. Crowley's failure to help with the rescue effort ruined his reputation as a climber.[20] Between these deaths and his failure to reach the peak, Crowley would never climb again.

The A∴A∴

Crowley took Rose and their infant daughter along on other adventures in 1906, including a trek across southern China. During this time, he began daily recitations of the Augoeides invocation,[21] which he thought would eventually unite him with his Holy Guardian Angel—the quintessential goal of magick. He experienced several revelations during this trip, including attaining the grade of Exempt Adept $7° = 4^\square$ and realizing that the gods had a plan

---

19 Wells, Colin. "Something Wicked This Way Comes." *Rock and Ice*, 136 (September 2004):60.

20 Whether he bitterly felt the mutineers got what they deserved, or whether he didn't realize exactly what had happened until morning, is unclear from Crowley's account.

21 The Greek *Augoeides* (lit. "Shining Image") is a Neoplatonic term for the body of light known to advanced initiates; Crowley came to identify this term with the Holy Guardian Angel. Although the invocation itself is from a Greek magical papyrus in the British Museum, Crowley inserted it as a "preliminary invocation" to his edition of *The Goetia* (1904) and later based his "Liber Samekh" upon it. See the second, illustrated edition of *The Goetia*.

for him.[22] Taking a separate route home from his family, Crowley arrived in England to find news that his infant daughter had died of typhoid, and that Rose had sunken into alcoholism. With his personal life in ruin, he sought understanding through magick, and concluded that the gods were punishing him for shirking his duties as their chosen prophet.

Crowley became ill and went to stay with his friend and G.D. mentor, George Cecil Jones (Frater D.D.S.). He describes what happened next in "Liber LXI vel Causae" (the history lection):

> 19. Returning to England, he laid his achievements humbly at the feet of a certain adept D.D.S., who welcomed him brotherly and admitted his title to the grade which he had so hardly won.
>
> 20. Thereupon these two adepts conferred together, saying: May it not be written that the tribulations shall be shortened? Wherefore they resolved to establish a new Order which should be free from the errors and deceits of the former one.
>
> 21. Without Authority they could not do this, exalted as their rank was among adepts. They resolved to prepare all things, great and small, against that day when such Authority should be received by them, since they knew not where to seek for higher adepts than themselves, but knew that the true way to attract the notice of such was to equilibrate the symbols. The temple must be builded before the God can indwell it.

They were joined by Captain (later Major-General) J.F.C. Fuller (Frater N.S.F. [1878–1966]).[23] Fuller had entered the contest for the "best essay on the works of Aleister Crowley," which Crowley had sponsored to promote his three-volume *Collected Works*; being the only entrant, Fuller won. He had studied yoga while stationed abroad, and had a keen interest in all things occult. To quote "Liber Causae" again:

> 27. In the fullness of time, even as a blossoming tree that beareth fruit in its season, all these pains were ended, and these

---

22 This occurred when he fell off his horse, tumbled down a ravine, and marveled at how he possibly could have survived. For the grade of Exempt Adept, see Chapter 2 on A∴A∴.

23 Fuller's motto *Non Sine Fulmine* is Latin for "Not without a thunderbolt."

adepts and their companions obtained the reward which they had sought—they were to be admitted to the Eternal and Invisible Order that hath no name among men.

Crowley immediately launched an ambitious publication schedule of the official organ of A∴A∴, *The Equinox*, which appeared at six-month intervals for five years, between 1909 and 1913.

Membership thrived during the first years of *The Equinox*'s publication, spurred in part by publicity from Mathers' failed injunction to prevent Crowley from publishing the Golden Dawn's rituals. The press proved to be a double-edged sword, however, when it panned *The Rites of Eleusis*. This daring performance series (one for each of the seven planets) blended sacred poetry, music, and dance, and was presented on consecutive Wednesdays at London's Caxton Hall in October and November 1910. The yellow press seized the opportunity to dredge up whatever dirt they could on Crowley: from his divorce from Rose to his rumored homosexuality, all was fair game. Where the facts were insufficient, rumor, gossip, and fiction ruled the day. The negative press about Crowley, his friends, and their cult of immorality—coupled with Crowley's reluctance to defend himself and his circle—drove away many members, including A∴A∴ charter members J.F.C. Fuller and George Cecil Jones,[24] leaving behind but a dedicated core.

The O.T.O.

The *Book of Lies* (1912) was an exercise in writing 93 brief and unrelated chapters of magical instruction whose contents were dictated by their chapter number. "I wrote one or more daily at lunch or dinner by the aid of the god Dionysus," Crowley recalled coyly in his *Confessions*.[25] Yet one of these chapters raised the ire of Theodor Reuss, head of Ordo Templi Orientis, as it revealed in plain language the Order's central secret. When Reuss came calling, Crowley claimed ignorance and blamed it on the wine. However, once he realized what the secret was, it changed his life forever.

---

24 Jones unsuccessfully sued *The Looking Glass* newspaper for libel; see Kaczynski, *Perdurabo Outtakes*. Crowley's relationship with the British press is thoroughly examined in Stephensen, P.R., and Crowley, A., *The Legend of Aleister Crowley: A Study of the Facts*, with an introduction by Stephen J. King, Enmore, New South Wales: Helios Books, 2007.
25 p. 709.

The Guardian of the Flame.

Photo of Crowley from the Rites of Eleusis
publicity booklet (1910)

Arguably, the only event more profound for him in his life was receiving *The Book of the Law*. Reuss appointed Crowley the British head of the Oriental Templars, with the title "Supreme and Holy King of Ireland, Iona, and all the Britains." For this role, Crowley chose the magical name Baphomet—after the goat-headed god for which the Templars were burnt as heretics for worshipping.[26]

Crowley energized the O.T.O. in a way that Reuss seemed unable to do. He revised the English rituals to conform with *The*

---

26 As of this writing, the Vatican has announced publication of documentation of the Templars' trial, noting that it exonerates them of any heresies.

Book of the Law and soon began performing O.T.O. initiations. Crowley succeeded Reuss as Outer Head of the Order on Reuss's death in 1923.

America

When World War I broke out in England in 1914, Crowley moved to America. This he did for several reasons. First, he had spent his inheritance on self-publishing, travel, mountaineering, and other luxuries, and hoped desperately that New York lawyer and patron of the arts John Quinn (1870–1924) would be interested in purchasing one-of-a-kind editions of Crowley's works. (Quinn would buy only a few of Crowley's books.) Second, he had offered his services to the British military but had been turned down. Crowley believed that he could help his country by infiltrating the German propaganda machine in the U.S., discrediting them, and helping to bring America into the war on England's side. This scheme required him to behave like a traitor, posing as an Irish nationalist, publicly burning his British passport, and writing over-the-top anti-British propaganda. Many dismissed Crowley's claim to being an agent as nothing more than disingenuous backpedaling after he realized he'd backed the wrong horse. However, considerable evidence suggests that he indeed acted with the knowledge of authorities in both America and England, and this is confirmed in U.S. military intelligence files. When, on February 2, 1917, the U.S. broke off diplomatic ties with Germany (as a prelude to declaring war), Crowley wrote in his diary, "My 2¼ years' work crowned with success."[27]

While in the U.S., Crowley seized the opportunity to sell more books, begin publishing a new edition of *The Equinox*, and try to establish an O.T.O. body. While he wasn't very successful in any of these endeavors, he underwent a months-long process of initiation from which he emerged as the Magus *To Mega Therion* (the Great Beast), his seat as a Master of the Temple filled by his Magical Son and heir apparent, Charles Stansfeld Jones (1886–1950),

---

27 *Perdurabo*, p. 230. For a thorough examination of Crowley's intelligence claims, see Spence, Richard B., *Secret Agent 666: Aleister Crowley, British Intelligence and the Occult*, Port Townsend, WA: Feral House, 2008; Spence, "Secret Agent 666: Aleister Crowley and British intelligence in America, 1914–1918." *International Journal of Intelligence and CounterIntelligence*, 13 no. 3 (2000):359–71. Additional information appears in *The Legend of Aleister Crowley* (2007), p. 16.

better known by his occult nom de plume, Frater Achad. Jones was a brilliant and gifted student who helped Crowley to decipher some of the more cryptic passages of *The Book of the Law*, and who served as his "field organizer" for a fledgling O.T.O. group in Detroit. Although they later fell out, Jones continued to take on students and reference Crowley extensively in his own books *QBL or the Bride's Reception* (1922), *The Egyptian Revival* (1923), *The Chalice of Ecstasy* (1923), *Crystal Vision through Crystal Gazing* (1923), and *The Anatomy of the Body of God* (1925).

The Abbey of Thelema

When hostilities ended in Europe, Crowley and his then-Scarlet Woman,[28] New York school teacher Leah Hirsig (1883–1975), made their way to Cefalù, Sicily, to establish a Thelemic commune. He dubbed it the Abbey of Thelema after the *Gargantua and Pantagruel* of François Rabelais (ca. 1495–1553). Life there was devoted to magick, with a daily routine of ritual and study for all who cared to visit—and an assorted group of bohemians, eccentrics, and occultists did indeed visit. Some—like the American character actress Jane Wolfe (1875–1958)[29] and Australian O.T.O. Viceroy (organizer) Frank Bennett (1868–1930)—were so profoundly changed by the visit that they spent the rest of their lives representing Crowley, Thelema, the A∴A∴, and O.T.O. Others, like writer Mary Butts (1890–1937) and her lover Cecil Maitland (1892–1926), returned to London "looking like ghosts."[30] The most tragic tale, however, belongs to Oxford student Frederick Charles

---

28 The Scarlet Woman is an office first mentioned in *The Book of the Law,* I:15, "Now ye shall know that the chosen priest & apostle of infinite space is the prince-priest the Beast; and in his woman called the Scarlet Woman is all power given. They shall gather my children into their fold: they shall bring the glory of the stars into the hearts of men." In "One Star in Sight" (see page 93 *infra*), Crowley writes of members of A∴A∴ that, "They must acknowledge the Authority of the Beast 666 and of the Scarlet Woman as in the book it is defined, and accept Their Will as concentrating the Will of our Whole Order." He footnotes this and explains further, "'Their Will'— not, of course, their wishes as individual human beings, but their will as officers of the New Aeon."

29 Perhaps best remembered for her role in Mary Pickford's *Rebecca of Sunnybrook Farm* (1917).

30 Hamnett, Nina. *Laughing Torso.* London: Constable & Co, 1932, p. 177. The Butts diaries in Yale University's Beinecke Rare Book Room

"Raoul" Loveday (1900–1923): a bright and promising disciple who quickly became very dear to Crowley, he died after drinking contaminated spring water while staying at the Abbey. Loveday's grief-stricken and embittered widow Betty May (b. 1893) returned to London and sold the tabloids an outrageous tale of how Raoul died from drinking the blood of a cat sacrificed during an infernal ritual. The London press unleashed the full force of its pen upon Crowley, branding him with his now-infamous title of "The Wickedest Man in the World." Crowley lacked the funds to return to London and defend himself, so he frustratedly watched the press clippings mount until the government finally asked him to leave Italy.[31]

Crowley on Drugs

While living at the Abbey, Crowley contributed several articles to *The English Review* under various pseudonyms. Two of these, "The Great Drug Delusion" and "The Drug Panic," described Crowley's attitudes on drug legalization and his emerging theory of addiction. Crowley had experimented with the magical use of drugs, most of which he acquired legally from his chemist. He also experimented with the mescal cactus and its psychoactive effects while climbing mountains in Mexico in 1900. England's passage of the Dangerous Drugs Act in 1920, however, changed things for the worse for him. He had developed severe asthma as a result of his high-altitude climbs. In 1919, his physician prescribed heroin as an analgesic and antispasmodic. With the Dangerous Drugs Act, Crowley was one of many people who were physically dependent on a medicine they could no longer purchase legally. His efforts to wean himself[32] prompted a great deal of self-reflection, from

---

(General MSS 487) recount the magical work she did at the Abbey of Thelema.

31 There is more to Crowley's expulsion from Italy than simply bad press, including internecine Masonic rivalry and the widespread expulsion of expatriates following Mussolini's rise to power.

32 His diary *The Fountain of Hyacinth* (a.k.a. *Liber Nike,* after the Greek goddess of victory) shows that he wasn't entirely successful in his attempts. Part-published in various places, the full diary appears in *Crowley on Drugs* (forthcoming). Because so much has been made of Crowley's heroin addiction, it is worth noting that Crowley became free of the drug in 1924, and did not use it again until 1940, when it was again prescribed to treat

which emerged his theory of addiction. Recreational drug use, lacking purpose, is ultimately hedonistic and leads to dependence; but use directed toward the accomplishment of one's True Will, by virtue of keeping a higher purpose ever in mind, protects one from addiction.

Crowley pitched a novel based on these principles to book publisher William Collins, who contracted the title. Amazingly, he dictated the entirety of *The Diary of a Drug Fiend* in twenty-eight days. It tells the story of the protagonist's life in England's drug underground, his meeting the wise and enigmatic King Lamus (Crowley), and his redemption and recovery at the Abbey of Thelema. Not only was it a novel, it was an advertisement for the Abbey as a drug rehabilitation clinic. The release of this controversially-titled book was greeted by the press with the outcry that was now customary for Crowley: *The Sunday Express* called it "A Book for Burning."[33] Collins quietly let the first edition sell out without printing any further copies.

Magick in Theory and Practice

Following Crowley's 1923 expulsion from Italy, the Abbey of Thelema eventually closed as its residents gradually drifted away. Crowley wandered around the region, including Tunisia, Germany, and France. Settling for a time in Paris with his new secretary, Francis Israel Regardie (1907–1985), and a new student, Gerald Yorke (1901–1983), he set his sights on publishing his magnum opus, *Magick in Theory and Practice* (1929–1930). It was part three of a four-part series he called *Book Four* or *Liber ABA*. The first two parts he had written in 1911 and 1912 under orders from an entity called Ab-ul-diz, whom he and Mary Desti (a.k.a. Mary d'Este Sturges [1871–1931]) had contacted during a magical working in Switzerland. As with much of Crowley's work, this third part had been around in outline and draft form for years. It was the basis for a series of classes on magick that he taught in the U.S., and Mary Butts helped Crowley with it while staying at the Abbey of Thelema. The book garnered positive reviews; even his former

---

his asthma. He received government-controlled medicinal doses by mail until his death in 1947. Frequent descriptions of Crowley as a lifelong drug addict are false.

33 November 19, 1922.

The rare dust wrapper to The Diary of a Drug Fiend *(1922).*
Picture credit: Anthony W. Iannotti.

student Victor Neuburg gave it a glowing recommendation in the *Sunday Referee.*

Encouraged by this new success, Crowley returned to England. He was soon signed by P.R. Stephensen to the Mandrake Press, which launched a campaign to rehabilitate his reputation and promote a series of new titles. These included a short-story collection, *The Stratagem and Other Stories* (1929), his novel *Moonchild* (1929), and the first two volumes of his six-volume *Confessions* (1929). Stephensen also defended Mandrake's new author in *The Legend of Aleister Crowley* (1930), an exposure of Crowley's mistreatment in the press and a defense of his body of work.

Spurred on by Mandrake's efforts, Crowley successfully sued a London bookseller for libel for advertising a copy of *The Diary of a Drug Fiend* as "withdrawn from circulation." This encouraged him to attempt other lawsuits against acquaintances whose memoirs offended him, including Ethel Mannin's *Confessions and Impressions* (1930) and Nina Hamnett's *Laughing Torso* (1932). These suits not only failed, they attracted a long line of creditors who were finally able to locate Crowley and bring him before the Official Receiver. In 1935, he was forced into bankruptcy.

During the 1930s and '40s, a group of devoted Thelemites in California operated the only active Thelemic O.T.O. body in the world. Agape Lodge conducted initiations, printed an edition of *The Book of the Law*, collected donations for Crowley's publishing efforts, and even sent him gifts of chocolates and Perique tobacco during World War II. One of the members, Captain (later Major) Grady Louis McMurtry (1918–1985), met Crowley while stationed in Europe during the war. Crowley was so impressed with this young man that he elevated him to IX° and made him his envoy, empowering him to take control of the O.T.O. in California and the U.S. if circumstances ever warranted it. McMurtry was instrumental in reviving the O.T.O. when it became moribund following the death of Crowley's successor, Karl Germer (1885–1962).

In his twilight years, Crowley proved as prolific as ever. His books *Little Essays Toward Truth* (1938) and *Eight Lectures on Yoga* (1939) are true gems of understated wisdom and clarity. He then spent five years collaborating with student and artist Frieda Lady Harris (1877–1962) to design a new tarot deck and its companion volume, *The Book of Thoth* (1944). The deck is a masterpiece, each card dense with layers of symbolism that keep emerging even after years of study; it remains one of the best-selling tarot decks in the world to this day. *The Book of Thoth* is no less magisterial, condensing forty-five years of occult study and practice into his most mature book on magick. Crowley next released *Olla: An Anthology of 60 Years of Song* (1946), a hand-picked selection of his best poetry. He rightfully remarked at the time, "I doubt whether anyone else can boast—if it is a boast—of 60 years of song."[34]

Aleister Crowley died on December 1, 1947, with chronic bronchitis finally taking its toll on his heart. Although he had been living in a boarding house—with a nurse available at the end only through the generosity of Frieda Harris—he died with four hundred British pounds in a strongbox under his bed, earmarked for

---

34 *Perdurabo*, p. 447.

the O.T.O.'s publication of *Liber Aleph* and *Magick without Tears*. Until the day he died, Crowley never wavered in dedication to his mission as prophet of the Law of Thelema.

Recommended Reading

Crowley's body of work is so large that it's hard to know where to begin. I've selected a "top eleven" list of books on magick that are essential reading for anyone who wishes to further study Thelema. In addition to the works listed below, my own biography, *Perdurabo*, provides a detailed look at his life.

Among his unique accomplishments, Crowley developed a system of classification for his writings that provides guidance to students of the value he placed on each of his books, and the states of mind he experienced during the process of writing them.

- Class A consists of books or writings that may not be changed in as much as the style of a letter. They represent the utterance of an Adept beyond the criticism of even the Visible Head of the Order.
- Class B are books or essays that are the result of ordinary scholarship, enlightened, and, earnest.
- Class C writings are to be regarded as suggestive rather than anything else.
- Class D refers to Official Rituals and Instructions.
- Class E refers to promulgations, manifestos, and other public statements.
- Some publications are composite and pertain to more than one class.

Regarding the classifications of the books listed below: Many include writings in various classes, such as *The Equinox* and *Liber ABA*. Some are modern compilations of Crowley's writings, such as *The Revival of Magick*. We do not assign classes to edited collections.

> *777 and Other Qabalistic Writings*: Crowley's important writings on the Qabalah collected in one place. (777 itself is in Class B.)
> *The Book of Lies*: Endlessly entertaining and enlightening. (Class C.)

The Book of Thoth: Crowley's last word on magick, an indispensable guide to his tarot deck. (Class B.)

Eight Lectures on Yoga: Perhaps the clearest explanation of yoga ever written. (Class B.)

The Equinox: This is really ten books (eleven with the "Blue" Equinox). You can also get *Gems from the Equinox*, which includes most of the key libri (books) from *The Equinox*.

The Equinox III(9): The Holy Books of Thelema. The indispensable and accurate modern collection of the major Class A writings that define the spiritual system of Thelema. (Parenthetically, *The Book of the Law* appears twice. The typeset version is called *Liber 220*, while the handwritten manuscript is *Liber 31*.)

The Equinox III(10): Sold separately from *The Equinox* set, this modern volume collects the foundational documents of the O.T.O.

The Law is for All: Edited by Louis Wilkinson, this is Crowley's "authorized" verse-by-verse commentary on *The Book of the Law*.

Liber Aleph: This collection of letters to Crowley's Magical Son, Frater Achad, delves into some of the deepest mysteries of magick, sex, Thelema, and the Gnostic Mass. (Class B.)

Magick: Liber ABA, Book Four: If you buy only one book on this list, this is it. Crowley's masterwork on magick, with enough libri in the appendices to keep you busy for a lifetime. This modern collection, edited by O.T.O. Frater Superior Hymenaeus Beta, includes *Book IV, Part 1: Mysticism; Book IV, Part 2: Magick; Book IV, Part 3: Magick in Theory and Practice;* and *Book IV, Part 4: The Equinox of the Gods*. A great many supplemental writings are included as well. It is extensively illustrated, annotated, and indexed for exceptional ease of use.

The Revival of Magick and Other Essays: A delightful introduction to Crowley's philosophy, this is a collection of essays in which Crowley clearly explains magick and Thelema in nontechnical language for a lay audience.

PART ONE

MYSTICAL AND MAGICAL SOCIETIES

CHAPTER TWO

A∴A∴

> This community of light has existed since the first day of the world's creation, and its duration will be to the end of time. It is the society of those elect who know the Light in the Darkness and separate what is pure therein.
>
> This community possesses a School, in which all who thirst for knowledge are instructed by the Spirit of Wisdom itself; and all the mysteries of God and of nature are preserved therein for the children of light. Perfect knowledge of God, of nature, and of humanity are the objects of instruction in this school.
>
> —*The Cloud Upon the Sanctuary,* von Eckartshausen

THE WESTERN MYSTERY TRADITION states that a universal teaching underlies the world's diverse religions. This teaching has been passed down from time immemorial by illuminated teachers—whether called Secret Chiefs (in the Golden Dawn) or Mahatmas (in the Theosophical Society) or the Great White Brotherhood (in many occult traditions). These Adepts have withdrawn from the world to their hidden mansions to perform their duty—which is nothing less than directing the spiritual evolution of the human race. Below them is a succession of leaders and teachers who convey their recondite knowledge to seekers lucky or persistent enough to locate a willing introducer.

For Crowley, the "invisible college" whose curriculum specifically teaches and examines students in the Wisdom Teachings is

A∴A∴[1] (The name of the Order is never disclosed to the profane.) In contrast with O.T.O., where initiates function as a magical, social, and even political group,[2] the work of A∴A∴ is primarily solitary. The initiate has contact with his mentor and, later, his own students (should he be authorized to admit them), and few others. The curriculum concerns the development of the individual and preparation for the discovery and performance of the True Will. Members may not advance until they have trained another to fill the grade about to be vacated; thus, there is an unbroken student-teacher chain from the top of the Order down.

Like any other college, members must pass rigorous exams. And they *are* rigorous: For example, here are sample questions from the 1945 Students' examination given by Crowley to Kenneth Grant:

- Buddhism may be divided into these classes: 1) Hinayana (Burma, Siam, Ceylon), 2) Mahayana (Tibet), 3) Twelve sects in Japan, 4) Chinese Buddhism. What divisions of Christianity correspond to each, and why?
- Reconcile the two apparently conflicting series of meanings of the number 65.
- Describe a woman with Uranus conjunct Moon trine Venus rising in 8° Capricorn.[3]

Understandably, of some sixty Probationers admitted to the A∴A∴ during the first five-year publication cycle of *The Equinox,* only eight passed to the first grade of Neophyte.

The following table gives the grade structure of the A∴A∴, beginning with Student and ending with Ipsissimus. The grade symbols, and most of the degree names, come directly from its predecessor organizations, including the Golden Dawn and Societas Rosicruciana. The first number gives the ordinal grade (1st, 2nd, 3rd, etc.), while the second number gives the corresponding *Sephira* (or number) on the Tree of Life (see Chapter Five). Just as the Tree of Life diagrams the process of creation according to the Qabalah, this same diagram also serves as a roadmap for attainment in

---

1 The three dots arranged in the shape of a triangle is a common Masonic symbol indicating the abbreviation of a sacred word or concept.

2 By political I refer to its goal of promulgating the Law of Thelema to the polity, or public at large.

3 Grant, Kenneth. *Remembering Aleister Crowley*. London: Skoob Books, 1991, p. 52.

A∴A∴. Initiates symbolically begin at the tenth and final sephira, called *Malkhuth* (kingdom), and ascend to the first, *Kether* (crown). Thus, the Neophyte grade 1°=10□ is the first grade in A∴A∴, corresponding to the tenth sephira. The figure on page 40 shows these grades on the Tree of Life for clarity.

Degree System of the A∴A∴

The Order of the S.S.		
10°=1□	Ipsissimus	
9°=2□	Magus	
8°=3□	Magister Templi	Master of the Temple
—	Babe of the Abyss	
The Order of the R.C.		
7°=4□	Adeptus Exemptus	Exempt Adept
6°=5□	Adeptus Major	Major Adept
5°=6□	Adeptus Minor	Minor Adept
—	Dominus Liminis	Master of the Threshold
The Order of the G.D.		
4°=7□	Philosophus	
3°=8□	Practicus	
2°=9□	Zelator	
1°=10·	Neophyte	
Without		
0°=0□	Probationer	
—	Student	

Grade System

The A∴A∴ grade system may be studied in "One Star in Sight,"[4] "Liber Collegii Sancti" (Liber 185), "Liber XIII vel Graduum Montis Abiegni," "Liber A vel Armorum" (Liber 312), "Liber Tau" (Liber 400), and "Liber Viarum Viae" (Liber 868). Since virtually all of the A∴A∴ instructional papers are published, one could theoretically pursue a course of independent study. However, most people lack the objectivity to critically evaluate their own work. A∴A∴ provides contact with both a mentor and a magical current, and the opportunity for service to humanity and one's students.

Before applying to A∴A∴, a student is expected to have studied some fundamental materials in religion, philosophy, and

4 See Appendix I.

science, much as a high school student will take college prep courses before applying. The recommended reading list, published in *Liber ABA* and elsewhere, covers an array of topics, including magick, Eastern and Western mysticism, philosophy, and even the hard and soft sciences. Once versed in the fundamentals, students wishing to join the Order may write to the Cancellarius (or Chancellor)[5] who will assist them in receiving the Student Examination. According to Crowley, "The first condition of membership in A∴A∴ is that one is sworn to identify one's own Great Work with that of raising mankind to higher levels, spiritually, and in every other way."[6] If the Student is to be admitted, he or she will swear the Oath of a Probationer and begin the Task as outlined in "Liber 185."

The "outer order," to which Crowley gave the initials G.D., differed from the Order of the Golden Dawn in several significant ways. Whereas the Golden Dawn's outer order merely instructed and prepared students for doing magic in the "inner order," students in Crowley's system do both magick and yoga from the outset. The initiate works through the four elemental grades, designing and manufacturing the corresponding symbolic elemental tools (or "weapons"). Concurrently, he or she practices progressively more demanding exercises in yoga and meditation, achieving mastery of both body and mind. The curriculum also trains initiates to master banishing rituals and astral projection (Neophyte), hatha and raja yoga (Zelator), divination and Qabalah (Practicus), evocation and devotion (Philosophus).

Some Tasks of the G.D.

Grade	Element	Magical Weapon	Yogic Practice
Neophyte	Earth	Pentacle	Liber E
Zelator	Air	Dagger/Sword	Asana, Pranayama
Practicus	Water	Chalice/Cup	Gnana Yoga
Philosophus	Fire	Wand	Mahasatipatthana

In combination, these disciplines leave the initiate at the threshold of the second order, duly prepared for the work of the Adeptus Minor, which is to enter into the Knowledge and Conversation of

---

5 The contact address is provided in Appendix IV.
6 *Magick without Tears*, letter 9.

the Holy Guardian Angel (H.G.A.). The identity of the Angel is a great mystery.

Crowley hinted at the nature of the Angel's relation to the aspirant in several of his writings, among which is the following:

> This then is the true aim of the Adept in this whole operation, to assimilate himself to his Angel by continual conscious communion. For his Angel is an intelligible image of his own true Will, to do which is the whole of the law of his Being.
>
> ... the Angel is in truth, the Logos or articulate expression of the whole Being of the Adept, so that as he increases in the perfect understanding of His name, he approaches the solution of the ultimate problem, Who he truly is.[7]

He further stated,

> One must nevertheless persist, aspiring with ardor towards one's Angel, and comforted by the assurance that He is guiding one secretly towards Himself, and that all one's mistakes are necessary preparations for the appointed hour of meeting Him. Each mistake is the combing-out of some tangle in the hair of the bride as she is being coiffed for marriage.[8]

Members of the Second Order perfect their magick, becoming Major and Exempt Adepts along the way. Exempt Adepts demonstrate their learning by writing a thesis that outlines their understanding of how the magical universe works. Crowley identifies not only Éliphas Lévi's *Clef des Grands Mystères* (*Key of the Mysteries*) as an example of such an essay, but also Isaac Newton's *Principia*.

Having attained the heights of the Second Order, a terrible ordeal confronts the Adept, the Ordeal of the Abyss. It is inevitable and inexorable, for taking the first step on the path of initiation requires the magician to see the journey through to its end—if not in this lifetime, then in another. To advance further involves the voluntary renunciation of all that one is, all attainments (even the H.G.A.), and all sense of self. If the magician refuses to release these things, then the universe will take them away by force, for the Third

---

7 *Magick in Theory and Practice*, Appendix IV, "Liber Samekh," pp. 300–1.

8 *Magick in Theory and Practice*, "Chapter XVIII, Of Clairvoyance and of the Body of Light," pp. 170–1.

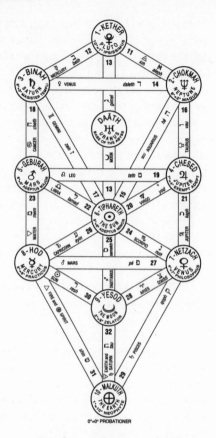

Grades on the Tree of Life

Order concerns itself not with personal attainment, but with the spiritual development of the human race.

A great Abyss, the gulf between the realms of Reason and the Divine, spans the road ahead. Herein lies Choronzon, the demon of dispersion, the absence of coherent form, the metaphysical contrary to the entire process of magick. Herein also lie the Black Brothers— the failed magicians who are unable to relinquish their hold on material things, their egos, or their power; who, instead of crossing the Abyss, become mired like Mastodons in a tar pit, setting themselves up as false and degenerate gods.

The Babe of the Abyss is he or she who successfully passes through this Ordeal and achieves the Sephirah of Binah. Crowley here invokes the image of the Cup of Babalon. In the Thelemic canon, Babalon is the Universal Lover, accepting all that one is, every last drop of blood, into her Cup, the Holy Graal. For only as a desiccated corpse, incinerated by passionate union with her, is the remaining ash light enough to be carried on the winds across the Abyss, to be reborn in Binah.

Being reconstituted in Binah, the City of the Pyramids, the Magister Templi or Master of the Temple has undergone, in Crowley's words, "the perfect annihilation of that personality which limits and oppresses his true self,"[9] and is at one with the universe, tending to his or her garden of disciples. Further renunciation soon becomes necessary, and the Master of the Temple must renounce unity with the universe in order to reformulate a new ego based on all that has been learned up to this point. As Magus, or Logos, he vibrates a unique Word whose utterance symbolically destroys the world in fire. Speaking literally, the Magus creates a new magical current that will forever change the world. In *The Book of Lies*, Crowley identifies seven Magi who have thus shaped history with their "word": Lao Tzu (Taoism), Siddhartha (Buddhism), Krishna (Hinduism), Tahuti (Hermeticism), Moses (Judaism), Dionysus (one of many dying and resurrected gods exemplified by Christianity), Mohammed (Islam), and himself (Thelema).[10]

All that remains after this is the grade of Ipsissimus, who is "pre-eminently the Master of all modes of existence; that is, his being is entirely free from internal or external necessity." Crowley defined this with *anatta* or *anatman* (literally "non-self"), a Buddhist technical term indicating "the absence of limiting self-identity in people and things."[11] The Ipsissimus has mastered the process of thesis-antithesis-synthesis—uniting being, nonbeing, and becoming, and action, nonaction, and tendency-to-action—and is free of any limitation. Traditionally, an Ipsissimus is bound never to reveal this attainment to anyone other than the witness in whose presence he has accepted the grade.

In Appendix I, we have reproduced Crowley's description of A∴A∴ as given in "One Star in Sight." It is his most clear and concise statement about the work and goals of the Order.

---

9 "One Star in Sight."

10 These are also the first seven saints in the Collects of the Gnostic Mass. Kaplan's *Sefer Yetzirah* and Woodroffe's *Garland of Letters* are wonderfully illuminating books when read in the context of magically (re)creating the world by uttering a word.

11 Rawson, Philip. *Sacred Tibet*. London: Thames and Hudson, 1991.

CHAPTER THREE

Ordo Templi Orientis
O.T.O.

HERE IS ONE of Crowley's most eloquent descriptions of the O.T.O. from a letter to one of his disciples in his later years:

System of the O.T.O.

Cara Soror,
    Do what thou wilt shall be the whole of the Law.

You inform me that the Earnest Inquirer of your ambit has been asking you to explain the difference between the A∴A∴ and the O.T.O.; and that although your own mind is perfectly clear about it, you find it impossible to induce a similar lucidity in his. You add that he is not (as one might at first suppose) a moron. And will I please do what I can about it?

Well, here's the essential difference *ab ovo usque ad mala*[1]; the A∴A∴ concerns the individual, his development, his initiation, his passage from "Student" to "Ipsissimus"; he has no contact of any kind with any other person except the Neophyte who introduces him, and any Student or Students whom he may, after becoming a Neophyte, introduce.

---

1 Latin for "from the egg to the apples" (i.e. from the first to the last course of a Roman dinner); from beginning to end. (*The Harper Dictionary of Foreign Terms.*)

The details of this Pilgrim's Progress are very fully set forth in One Star in Sight; and I should indeed be stupid and presumptuous to try to do better than that. But it is true that with regard to the O.T.O. there is no similar manual of instruction. In the Manifesto, and other Official Pronunciamenti, there are, it is true, what ought to be adequate data; but I quite understand that they are not as ordered and classified as one would wish; there is certainly room for a simple elementary account of the origins of the Order, of its principles, of its methods, of its design, of the Virtue of its successive Grades. This I will now try to supply, at least in a brief outline.

Let us begin at the beginning. What is a Dramatic Ritual? It is a celebration of the Adventures of the God whom it is intended to invoke. (*The Bacchae* of Euripides is a perfect example of this.) Now, in the O.T.O., the object of the ceremonies being the Initiation of the Candidate, it is he whose Path in Eternity is displayed in dramatic form.

What is the Path?

1. The Ego is attracted to the Solar System.
2. The Child experiences Birth.
3. The Man experiences Life.
4. He experiences Death.
5. He experiences the World beyond Death.
6. This entire cycle of Point-Events is withdrawn into Annihilation.

In the O.T.O. these successive stages are represented as follows:—

1.   0°   (Minerval)
2.   I°   (Initiation)
3.   II°   (Consecration)
4.   III°   (Devotion)
5.   IV°   (Perfection, or Exaltation)
6.   P.I.   (Perfect Initiate)

Of these Events of Stations upon the Path all but three (II°) are single critical experiences. We, however, are concerned mostly with the very varied experiences of Life.

All subsequent Degrees of the O.T.O. are accordingly elaborations of the II°, since in a single ceremony it is hardly possible to sketch, even in the briefest outline, the Teaching of Initiates with regard to Life. The Rituals V°–IX° are then instructions to the Candidate how he should conduct himself; and they confer upon him, gradually, the Magical Secrets which make him Master of Life.

It is improper to disclose the nature of these ceremonies; firstly, because their Initiates are bound by the strictest vows not to do so; secondly, because surprise is an element in their efficacy; and thirdly, because the Magical Formulae explicitly or implicitly contained therein are, from a practical point of view, both powerful and dangerous.

...

Love is the law, love under will.

Fraternally,
666[2]

Ordo Templi Orientis, or the Order of Oriental Templars, is an esoteric, spiritual, and philosophical fraternity that uses a graded series of dramatic initiation rituals to teach men and women its core principles: individual liberty, self-discipline, self-knowledge, and universal fellowship. These initiations also reveal, gradually, O.T.O.'s central secret, which is commonly understood to be sex magick; however, the full meaning and practical application of this secret is only disclosed to initiates of its highest degree, the Sanctuary of the Gnosis.

Under Crowley's leadership, a primary function of O.T.O. became promulgation of the Law of Thelema and *The Book of the Law*. In addition to ceremonies of initiation, O.T.O. also provides its members with instruction, social events, rituals, and plays, and, if needed, guidance. It also engages in community service activities. Its teaching is syncretic, borrowing freely from multiple spiritual traditions. Crowley happily incorporated elements from Christianity, Buddhism, Hinduism, Judaism, and Islam; he wrote invocations to the Egyptian Isis, Greek Artemis, and Christian Mary. His successors at all levels of advancement strive for this kind of inclusiveness. In "Liber Librae,"[3] Crowley comments, "In true religion,

2 *Magick Without Tears*, A portion of Letter 13.
3 Found in *Magick*, *The Equinox*, and *Gems from the Equinox*.

there is no sect." For good reason, a common salutation in O.T.O. documents is "Peace, Tolerance, Truth."

While O.T.O.'s origins are rooted in nineteenth century esoteric Masonry, it differs from regular Freemasonry in several significant ways:

- Most important, O.T.O. makes no claim whatsoever to be Masonic, nor does it make Masons. It makes Magicians. In fact, many of the original rites concentrated in O.T.O. were (and continue to be) considered "irregular" or "clandestine"— and hence not recognized—by mainstream Freemasonry.
- In sharp contrast with Freemasonry, both men and women are admitted as members of O.T.O., with equal rights and privileges.
- Despite any similarity of form or titles, O.T.O.'s highest degrees—the VIII° and IX°—had, from the beginning, no official correlation with any other Masonic rite.

Degree Structure

The grade structure of O.T.O. consists of twelve degrees, divided into three grades or triads according to *The Book of the Law I:40*: "Who calls us Thelemites will do no wrong, if he look but close into the word. For there are therein Three Grades, the Hermit, and the Lover, and the man of Earth. Do what thou wilt shall be the whole of the Law." (Some degrees are considered introductory or pendant and not counted separately when referring to a triad.) As shown in the table below, the three triads are called Hermit, Lover and Man of Earth.

Man of Earth

The Man of Earth degrees are open to all men and women who meet the qualifications of being free, of full age, and of good report.

In the introductory, or Minerval, degree, the initiate is considered a guest and is not yet a full member. This guest status provides the initiate as much (or as little) time as he or she requires to decide whether or not to formally affiliate with O.T.O. in the I°. Here, the candidate "chooses to enter into relations with the solar

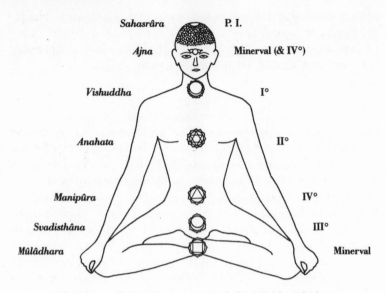

Sahasrâra · P. I.

Ajna · Minerval (& IV°)

Vishuddha · I°

Anahata · II°

Manipûra · IV°

Svadisthâna · III°

Mûlâdhara · Minerval

The Man of Earth Degrees and the Hindu Chakras

system. It incarnates."[4] At this point, the initiate becomes a Man and a Brother (modern Order leadership has added the terms Woman and Sister). Any time after the mandatory waiting periods have elapsed, the initiate is welcome to apply to the subsequent degrees of Magician (II°), Master Magician (III°), Perfect Magician (IV°) and Perfect Initiate (P.I.), where "the cycle is closed by the reabsorption of all individuality into infinity. It ends in absolute annihilation which ... may in reality be regarded ... as forming the starting point for new adventure of the same kind."[5]

In addition to symbolizing the soul's journey toward birth, life, death, and, ultimately, annihilation, the degrees also represent a journey through the chakras, or energy centers of the subtle body. Crowley attributed the Man of Earth degrees to the chakras as illustrated in the diagram above.

Subsequent advancement is by invitation only. The first of the invitational degrees is Knight of the East and West, which, according to "Liber CXCIV," "is but a bridge between the first and

---

4 *Confessions*, p. 701.
5 *Confessions*, p. 702.

second series; but it is important, for in that grade a new pledge-form must be signed, and the new Knight vowed to devote his life to the Establishment of the Law of Thelema." It is the gateway between the Man of Earth and Lover grades.

Lover

While members of the Man of Earth triad may hold office or assume responsibility in running the affairs of their local body, they take "no share in the Government of the Order" (Liber CXCIV). The Lover, however, takes oaths of service to the Order, enabling members to participate in its government. In the first of these degrees, the Sovereign Prince Rose-Croix (V°) is "responsible for all that concerns the Social Welfare of the Order. This grade is symbolically that of beauty and harmony; it is the natural stopping-place of the majority of men and women; for to proceed farther ... involves renunciation of the sternest kind" (CXCIV). The following degree, Knight of the Red Eagle (K.R.E.), designates members of the Senate, which includes lodge masters, honorary past masters, and members of the Electoral College. An Electoral College oversees the operations and welfare of the Man of Earth triad within its national borders. It is composed of eleven members who voluntarily renounce their own advancement during their eleven-year term of service.

Next follows the VI° or Illustrious Knight of the Order of Kadosch, "an executive or military body [that] represents the temporal power of the Supreme and Holy King" (CXCIV); the Grand Inquisitor Commander (G.I.C.) is entitled to a seat on the O.T.O. Grand Tribunal, which adjudicates all disputes and complaints unresolved by members of the V°; the Prince of the Royal Secret (P.R.S.) "is devoted to the Propagation of the Law in a very special manner; for this grade is the first in which the Beginning of the Inmost Secret is declared openly" (CXCIV).

Finally, members of the last grade of the Lover triad, the VII°, serve as Sovereign Grand Inspectors General of O.T.O. Members of this degree may also belong to the Supreme Grand Council, which oversees the affairs of the Lover triad much as the Electoral College oversees the affairs of the Man of Earth. In "Liber CXCIV," Crowley elaborates, "All members of the Seventh Degree travel as Sovereign Grand Inspectors General of the Order, and report, on their own initiative, to the Supreme and Most Holy King, as to the condition of all Lodges, and Chapters; to the Supreme Council, on all affairs of the Second Triad; and to the Electoral College, on those of the Third."

Hermit

Members of the VIII° are "fully instructed in the Principles of the Order, save in one point only," and "devote themselves to the understanding of what they have learned in their initiation" (CXCIV). Finally, in the IX°, or Sanctuary of the Gnosis, the secret is fully explained. Its members are devoted to studying and practicing "the theurgy and thaumaturgy of the grade," and, as further specified in "Liber CXCIV," "move unseen and unrecognized among the youngest of us, subtly and loftily leading us into the holy ineffable mysteries of the True Light." Furthermore, "they must be prepared to act as direct representatives of the Supreme and Most Holy King, radiating his light upon the whole world."

The grade of X° denotes the head of a Grand Lodge, which oversees a country. This officer—referred to by the titles National Grand Master General and Supreme and Holy King—has "ultimate responsibility for all within his holy kingdom" (CXCIV). Grand Masters are appointed by the Outer Head of the Order (O.H.O.). "Liber CXCIV" goes on to say, "Of the Eleventh Degree, its powers, privileges, and qualifications, nothing whatever is said in any grade. It has no relation to the general plan of the Order, is inscrutable, and dwells in its own Palaces." The XII° degree is reserved for the Outer Head of the Order, or Frater Superior.

Regarding Degrees in the O.T.O.

In *An Intimation with Reference to the Constitution of the Order*, Crowley stresses that "with us Government is Service, and nothing else." O.T.O. may be hierarchical, but the purpose of that hierarchy is not to set some people above others, but to place them in a position of service to assist newer members. As the U.S. Grand Master Sabazius said in his address to the 2001 E.v.[6] National O.T.O. Conference, "An O.T.O. degree is not a seal of attainment, it is an opportunity for attainment."

---

6 *Era vulgaris,* or "vulgar year," a Thelemic construct to denote that our calendar begins with the Supreme Ritual on March 20, 1904, counted as Year 0.

The Grade System of Ordo Templi Orientis

Grade	Degree	Title
The Third Triad: **Man of Earth**	0°	Minerval
	I°	Man and Brother, or Woman and Sister
	II°	Magician
	III°	Master Magician
	IV°	Perfect Magician and Companion of the Holy Royal Arch of Enoch
		Perfect Initiate, or Prince of Jerusalem
Outside all Triads		Knight of the East and West
The Second Triad: **Lover**	V°	Sovereign Prince(ess) Rose-Croix, and Knight (Dame Knight) of the Pelican and Eagle
		Knight of the Red Eagle, and Member of the Senate of Knight Hermetic Philosophers
	VI°	Illustrious Knight (Templar) of the Order of Kadosch, and Companion of the Holy Graal
		Grand Inquisitor Commander, and Member of the Grand Tribunal
		Prince of the Royal Secret
	VII°	Theoreticus, and Very Illustrious Sovereign Grand Inspector General
		Magus of Light, and Bishop of Ecclesia Gnostica Catholica
		Grandmaster of Light, and Inspector of Rites and Degrees
The First Triad: **Hermit**	VIII°	Perfect Pontiff of the Illuminati
		Epopt of the Illuminati
	IX°	Initiate of the Sanctuary of the Gnosis
	X°	Rex Summus Sanctissimus
	XI°	Initiate of the Eleventh Degree
	XII°	Frater Superior, and Outer Head of the Order

A list of official O.T.O. bodies may be found on the International Headquarters and Grand Lodge Web sites (see Appendix IV). We have also included (as Appendix II), "An Open Letter to Those Who May Wish to Join the Order" (Liber 101), Crowley's most enthusiastic and detailed description of his vision for the O.T.O.

CHAPTER FOUR

ECCLESIA GNOSTICA CATHOLICA—E.G.C.

THE E.G.C. MAY BE CONSIDERED the ecclesiastical arm of O.T.O. It is primarily dedicated to the performance of the Gnostic Mass, which includes the following proclamation of Thelemic religious doctrine.

The Creed

I believe in one secret and ineffable LORD; and in one Star in the Company of Stars of whose fire we are created, and to which we shall return; and in one Father of Life, Mystery of Mystery, in His name CHAOS, the sole viceregent of the Sun upon the Earth; and in one Air the nourisher of all that breathes.

And I believe in one Earth, the Mother of us all, and in one Womb wherein all men are begotten, and wherein they shall rest, Mystery of Mystery, in Her name BABALON.

And I believe in the Serpent and the Lion, Mystery of Mystery, in His name BAPHOMET.

And I believe in one Gnostic and Catholic Church of Light, Life, Love and Liberty, the Word of whose Law is THELEMA.

And I believe in the communion of Saints.

And, forasmuch as meat and drink are transmuted in us daily into spiritual substance, I believe in the Miracle of the Mass.

And I confess one Baptism of Wisdom whereby we accomplish the Miracle of Incarnation.

And I confess my life one, individual, and eternal that was, and is, and is to come.

AUMGN. AUMGN. AUMGN.

Ecclesia Gnostica Catholica (E.G.C.), or Gnostic Catholic Church, celebrates the Gnostic Mass, and offers other sacerdotal rites including baptism, confirmation, pubertal/menarcheal rites of passage, marriage, last rites, funerals, and requiems. Clergy are members of specific degrees within O.T.O.

The Gnostic Mass

Aleister Crowley wrote the Gnostic Mass in 1913 as an expression through dramatic ritual of the O.T.O.'s spiritual mysteries. Today, O.T.O. Oases and Lodges are charged with celebrating the Gnostic Mass on a regular basis. The rite calls for five officers: a Priest and Priestess representing the masculine and feminine polarities, a Deacon who oversees the ritual, assisting the clergy and guiding the congregation as needed, and two Children who carry implements and offer the sacraments to the congregants. In practice, the offices of the Children are often performed by adults, and when limited by practical circumstances, the rite can be performed with only three officers: Priest, Priestess and Deacon. Despite its resemblance to the Catholic Tridentine Mass (e.g. the Creed, Collects, and sacraments), the tenets and contents of the Gnostic Mass are profoundly Thelemic. Uniquely, each celebration of the Mass allows communicants to imbue their sacraments with a private intention, thus being active magicians rather than passive observers.[1] The ritual appears in many of Crowley's books, including *Magick, The Equinox* (vol. 3 nos. 1 and 10), *Gems from the Equinox*, and online at *www.hermetic.com/sabazius/gnostic_mass.htm* and *www.gnosticmass.org*.

Crowley penned the Mass soon after his June 1, 1912, appointment as O.T.O. National Grand Master for the U.K. As he recalled:

> My own relations with the Gnostic Catholic Church are like the annals of the poor, short and simple. My predecessor was rather keen about the Gnostics as the original founders of what, after many changes, has become the O.T.O. During my six weeks in Moscow in 1913 I had what I can only call almost continuous illumination and wrote some of my very best poems and essays there. Of course, the Gnostic Mass was one. It was inspired, I think, by Saint Basil's. It sounds rather extraordinary, but I seem to have had some premonition of the Revolution in Russia, and my idea was to write a Mass which would, in one sense, carry on the old tradition yet not come into conflict with science. The whole thing, as is almost

---

1 *Liber Aleph*, chapter 86 (Γη), "De Formula Tota."

invariably the case with my work, was written straight off in
white heat and never underwent revision.[1]

The Gnostic Mass presents, in stylized and dramatic form, the central secret of O.T.O. The ritual saw its first publication in 1918:
Crowley ran it in *The International*, an American journal he was
editing at the time. Theodor Reuss prepared a German translation
the same year. During this period, Crowley sought to establish a
U.S. Supreme Grand Council of O.T.O. in Detroit, with prospective
members preparing themselves with rehearsals of the newly published Gnostic Mass. Although the body never got off the ground,
the centrality of the Mass in Crowley's design indicates its importance to him. Reuss attended a 1920 International Masonic Conference in Zurich, where he proposed (alas, unsuccessfully) that the
Gnostic Mass be adopted as the official ritual of Rose Croix Freemasonry.

The Mass always remained part of Crowley's life: it was occasionally celebrated in the early 1920s at the Cefalù abbey,[2] and
he recited its Anthem at Raoul Loveday's funeral in 1923. When
recording selected poems in the 1940s, he included several of the
Collects from the Mass. Agape Lodge, founded in 1935 in southern California, began regular celebrations of the Gnostic Mass.
Today, its celebration serves as a primary objective for O.T.O. bodies worldwide, fulfilling Crowley's vision described in the *Confessions*.[3] Discussing the Anthem, he writes,

> The lyrical climax is in some respects my supreme achievement
> in invocation; in fact, the chorus beginning: "Thou who art
> I beyond all I am ..." seemed to me worthy to be introduced
> as the anthem into the Ritual of the Gnostic Catholic Church
> which, later in the year, I prepared for the use of the O.T.O.,
> *the central ritual of its public and private celebration*, corre-
> sponding to the Mass of the Roman Catholic Church. [italics
> added]

---

1 Crowley to W. B. Crow, 2 April 1945. Yorke Collection, Warburg Institute, University of London.

2 According to Crowley, "we occasionally celebrated a semi-religious ceremony known as the Gnostic Mass." See *The Legend of Aleister Crowley*
(3rd edition), p. 381.

3 *Confessions*, p. 714.

PART II

MYSTICISM AND MAGICK

CHAPTER FIVE

OVERVIEW OF MAGICK

DE CULTU (On Disciple)

Now, o my Son, that thou mayst be well guarded against thy
ghostly Enemies, do thou work constantly by the Means
prescribed in our Holy Books.

Neglect never the fourfold Adorations of the Sun in his four
Stations, for thereby thou doest affirm thy Place in Nature
and her Harmonies.

Neglect not the Performance of the Ritual of the Pentagram,
and of the Assumption of the Form of Hoor-pa-Kraat.

Neglect not the daily Miracle of the Mass, either by the Rite of
the Gnostic Catholic Church, or that of the Phœnix.

Neglect not the Performance of the Mass of the Holy Ghost, as
Nature herself prompteth thee.

Travel also much in the Empyrean in the Body of Light, seeking ever Abodes more fiery and lucid.

Finally, exercise constantly the Eight Limbs of Yoga. And so
shalt thou come to the End.

—*Liber Aleph*

WILL IS THE SOUL of Aleister Crowley's magical philosophy; his
famous definition of magick is "the Science and Art of causing
Change to occur in conformity with Will."[4] He named his system
Thelema after the Greek word for Will. Everyone has a *Will*—a
purpose, unique talent, calling, or function in the smooth running
of that magnificent cosmic machine which is the Universe. Magick
provides the tools to accomplish two things: First is to "know
thyself"—to use techniques like journaling, meditation, ritual, and
invocation to identify your personal strengths and successes—and

---

4 *Magick*, p. 126.

thereby discover your true Will. The second is to use these same tools to *accomplish* your Will.

Find your Will and do it. Sounds easy. But all the books written on magick; the varieties of magical and mystical systems through the millennia; the universities filled with college students wondering "What should I major in?"; the plethora of "self-help" books filling modern bookstores; and the workplaces occupied by people simply "getting by" in unfulfilling jobs, are all testimony to the fact that this is anything *but* easy. Crowley's innovation was to repurpose the traditions of magick to make this task more efficient.

Another of Crowley's innovations was to bring magick into the modern age. He coined the term "scientific illuminism" for his approach, which applies the scientific method to magick. This includes an emphasis on *reproducibility*. Rituals and exercises are performed precisely so that they can be replicated by others. Likewise, you should get clear and reproducible results with practice: If not, the particular ritual or exercise you're doing is (for you) merely superstition. To build a record of success, students first master these techniques in simple, mundane, and measurable goals before applying them to the higher purposes of magick.

Crowley also united the various systems of the East and West into a cohesive package. Magick recognizes certain universal truths contained within all religious and spiritual systems. Crowley attempted to extract that essence from the teachings of the world's varied schools of spiritual attainment. Building on an idea common in esoteric groups like the Theosophical Society and the Golden Dawn, he forged a particularly effective integration of Western magic, Eastern yoga, Qabalah, Hermeticism, Freemasonry, Rosicrucianism, and other mystery traditions throughout history.

Here follows a brief analysis of the major trends of spiritual development united in Crowley's system. Later we will look at the Holy Books he penned and some of their common themes.

Western Magic

Tribute and hyperbole are paid in equal measure to the medieval magical textbooks, called grammars or *grimoires*. These occult recipe books involve summoning angels (or demons) to do one's bidding—everything from making "three girls (or gentlemen) appear in your room after supper" to causing "Seething Water to come forth anon after thou hast put it in thy Hand." Much as we might like to see that last trick, we now live in more enlightened times— hopefully. Nevertheless, *grimoires* like the *Key of Solomon, Lesser Key of Solomon* (the *Goetia* or *Lemegeton*), *Grimoire of Armadel, Grimoire of Pope Honorius* and others still influence today's practices. These "forbidden books" give magick the following traditions:

- The invocation of divine authority into man to command spirits.
- The casting of the magical circle, surrounded with pentagrams or other protective symbols, within which the magician does all ritual.
- The doctrine that the planets rule certain days and hours of the day, dictating which times are best for which purposes (ideas carried over from astrology).
- The concept of the Great Magical Retirement (G.M.R.), or devoting a period of days, weeks, or months to physical and spiritual preparation for a ritual.
- The use of special ceremonial vestments (robe, crown, shoes, ring) and implements (dagger, salt, water, parchment, perfumes).

The present discussion is historical. Modern mystical and magical practices will be discussed in the next three chapters.

Two especially important traditions focus on angelic magic. One of these, *The Sacred Magic of Abramelin the Mage*, deals with how to contact one's Holy Guardian Angel (see Chapter 2). Another is the Enochian magic of Dr. John Dee (1527–1609) and Edward Kelly (1555–1597). The former was one of Europe's most learned men, court astrologer to Queen Elizabeth, a mathematician, cryptographer, and owner of England's largest private library. Kelly, on the other hand, was a convict and a spirit medium. Inspired by the apocryphal *Book of Enoch*, they summoned and conversed with angels, learning not only their magic but also their language, Enochian. These communications became the basis of the Enochian magic that played such a large role in the Golden Dawn, and in many of Crowely's writings, especially "A Brief Abstract Representation of the Universe" and *The Vision and the Voice*. The latter is the first recorded systematic exploration of Dee's Enochian Calls.

Qabalah

Long before a red string around the wrist signaled its entry into pop-culture trendiness, the Qabalah was already the heart and soul of the Western mystery tradition. More than the lingua franca of magick, its Tree of Life is the diagram of creation and the road map for attainment. The Qabalah is nothing less than the occult Rosetta stone: It translates the languages of astrology, tarot, mythology, and pretty much anything else you can imagine into a common vocabulary.

It's deceptively simple. In magick, the principle of *correspondence* says that like things go together: The planet Venus is named after a Roman goddess, who is also the Greek Aphrodite and the Norse Freya or Frigg, who gives her name to Friday (Freya's Day). She is also identified with the Egyptian Hathor, Netzach (Victory) on the Tree of Life, the Empress card of the Tarot, the Emerald, and the Rose. (See 777.)

One may not need Hebrew mysticism to make such lists, but the Qabalah's Tree of Life (illustrated on page 40) provides a handy way to keep them organized. The 10 Sephiroth and 22 interconnecting Paths can be written out as a thirty-two-item list. So long as our table is keyed to the organizational model of the Tree of Life diagram, we can put all our lists together and read *across* rather than down. In so doing, we see what ideas go together. Here are some examples of a few very important attributions collected together into tables that shed light on the esoteric meaning of a series of related symbols:

Ten Emanations or Sephiroth and the Ten Numbered Tarot Cards

Number	Sephira	Meaning	Attribution	Card
1	Kether	Crown	Primum Mobile*	Aces
2	Chokmah	Wisdom	Zodiac†	2s
3	Binah	Understanding	Saturn	3s
4	Chesed	Mercy	Jupiter	4s
5	Geburah	Strength	Mars	5s
6	Tiphereth	Beauty	Sun	6s
7	Netzach	Victory	Venus	7s
8	Hod	Splendor	Mercury	8s
9	Yesod	Foundation	Moon	9s
10	Malkuth	Kingdom	Material World	10s

* Later attributed to Pluto.
† Later attributed to Neptune.

Twenty-two Paths on the Tree of Life and the
Twenty-two Cards in the Major Arcana[5]

Path	Letter	Meaning	Attribution	Color	Tarot Card
11	א	Ox	Air	Pale yellow	Fool
12	ב	House	Mercury	Yellow	Magus
13	ג	Camel	Moon	Blue	Priestess
14	ד	Door	Venus	Emerald	Empress
15	ה	Window	Aquarius	Scarlet	Star
16	ו	Nail	Taurus	Red orange	Hierophant
17	ז	Sword	Gemini	Orange	Lovers
18	ח	Gate	Cancer	Amber	Chariot
19	ט	Serpent	Leo	Greenish yellow	Lust
20	י	Palm	Virgo	Yellowish green	Hermit
21	כ	Hand	Jupiter	Violet	Fortune
22	ל	Ox goad	Libra	Emerald	Adjustment
23	מ	Serpent	Water	Deep blue	Hanged Man
24	נ	Fish	Scorpio	Green blue	Death
25	ס	Prop	Sagittarius	Blue	Art
26	ע	Eye	Capricorn	Indigo	Devil
27	פ	Mouth	Mars	Scarlet	Tower
28	צ	Fish hook	Aries	Violet	Emperor
29	ק	Back of head	Pisces	Crimson (ultraviolet)	Moon
30	ר	Head	Sun	Orange	Sun
31	ש	Tooth	Fire	Orange scarlet	Aeon
32	ת	Tau	Earth	Indigo	Universe

Memorizing these connections may seem like a daunting task at first. Just remember that Crowley, upon joining the Golden Dawn, was bitterly disappointed that he was simply given the Hebrew alphabet to memorize, nothing more. Study and learn one column at a time. Only after you can close this book, write the numbers one

---

5 See 777 for these attributions. Note that this table reflects the *Hé* and *Tzaddi* switch as discussed in detail in *The Book of Thoth* and *Magick*.

through ten or eleven through thirty-two on a piece of paper and easily fill in their correspondences from memory should you move on to the next column. It will take time, but it will be well worth it: Crowley speaks in the language of Qabalistic correspondence, and you need to understand it thoroughly to get the most out of your magical studies.[6]

Templar/Mason/Rosicrucian Traditions

As discussed earlier, the magical groups championed by Aleister Crowley derive from eighteenth- and nineteenth-century secret societies like the Freemasons and the Rosicrucians. Some students find it helpful to read up on their heritage and place it in the larger context of popular fraternal groups of the era. It can also help to realize that the O.T.O. and A∴A∴ didn't appear fully formed in a vacuum but built on older traditions. The roots of the O.T.O. are entwined with numerous Masonic and quasi-Masonic groups like the Illuminati (0° and VIII°), Blue Lodge (I°–III°), Lodge of Perfection (IV°/P.I.) and Scottish Rite (V°–VII°), as well as more exotic rites like Memphis-Misraim, Martinism, and the Swedenborgian Rite. Likewise, A∴A∴ builds on the Golden Dawn model, which itself is an outgrowth of groups like Societas Rosicruciana in Anglia, the Society of Eight, the Fratres Lucis, and the Gold und Rosenkreuzers. While some may find history and legitimacy in tracing these roots, it isn't necessary to be a historian in order to be a magician.

Hermeticism/Gnosticism

The magical and theurgical traditions of second century Greece coalesced in various guises as Gnosticism, Neoplatonism, and Hermeticism. All these traditions work their way into Crowley's magical worldview. Golden Dawn founder William Wynn Westcott translated the *Chaldean Oracles* and similar texts of this period, which were incorporated into the Order's initiation rituals. Crowley frequently cites or paraphrases the *Chaldean Oracles* as well. Likewise, the *Goetia* that Crowley published (translated by Golden Dawn founder S. L. MacGregor Mathers) has prefixed to it a "Pre-

---

6 Dion Fortune's *Mystical Qabalah* is an excellent introduction to this subject.

liminary Invocation" which originates not from Solomonic tradition at all, but from a Graeco-Egyptian magical papyrus in the British Museum. Crowley thought this invocation so important that, dubbing it the *Augoeides* or "Bornless One," he analyzed it in "Liber Samekh" and used it as an invocation of his Holy Guardian Angel.

Another idea central to Crowley's system is that of Gnosis: That practitioners of magick can—and must—obtain meaningful insight into the divine through direct experience. Although the bulk of the known Gnostic texts were not discovered until 1945 at Nag Hammadi, enough was known to inspire the French Gnostic revival of the 1890s, from which the Ecclesia Gnostica Catholica emerged. As early as *The Sword of Song* (1904), Crowley referred to the *Codex Brucianus*, one of the Gnostic texts known in his time. Interestingly, the fundamental idea of Gnosticism—encountering the divine without the need for intermediaries—is not far removed from the Plymouth Brethren, who believed that any Christian, not just priests, can celebrate the Lord's Supper.

Egyptian Myth and Magick

The mythology and religion of Egypt made a profound impact on the culture of Crowley's generation, and the popular fascination with all things Egyptian shows no sign of waning today. In Crowley's day, the Rosetta stone had only recently unlocked the previously-indecipherable mysteries of Egyptian hieroglyphics.[7] Until that time, careless speculation filled in what was unknown about Egypt. This led to claims like that of Antoine Court de Gébelin (ca. 1719–1784), who wrote in *Le Monde Primitif* (1781), that the tarot derived from ancient pictograms of Egyptian initiatory rites; since the language had not yet been translated, nobody could say he was wrong.

While neither Crowley nor the Golden Dawn followed the Egyptian religious traditions per se, they assimilated names, ideas, and archetypes from the pantheons into their lexicon of symbolism. One of Crowley's most fundamental magical instructions, "Liber Resh" (see Chapter 6), involves addressing the sun four times daily with various appellations of the Egyptian sun god. Crowley's book

---

7 The stone was discovered by Napoleon's army in 1799, and in 1822 used by Jean-François Champollion to decipher Egyptian hieroglyphics.

on the tarot, *The Book of Thoth*, takes its name from the Egyptian god of magic and of writing. He named the "honeymoon," "burnout," and "second wind" phases of any undertaking (particularly magical work) after the gods Isis, Apophis, and Osiris, respectively: Isis is the Egyptian Venus, Apophis the adversary serpent who threatens to swallow the sun, and Osiris is the slain and resurrected god. These gods also serve as an arcanum for the Gnostic holy name IAO, which was itself the Greek version of the Hebrew *Yahweh* (YHVH).

Crowley named historical epochs (or spiritual dispensations) of mankind after the Egyptian divinities: Early matriarchal and fertility religions, of which the Venus of Willendorf is a popular archetype, he identified with the goddess Isis; the period dominated by slain and resurrected figures (including Jesus, Attis, Adonis, Dionysus, etc.) was named after Osiris; and the current era, the New Aeon of the Crowned and Conquering Child, or new age of mankind, after their child, Horus.

The most significant Egyptian connection to Thelema is, of course, the revelation of *The Book of the Law*. It is intimately associated with the Theban priest Ankh-f-n-Khonsu (ca. 725 B.C.E.), and its three chapters are attributed to three different Egyptian figures. Nuit is Infinite Space, the starry night sky. Hadit, the point of individuation, is depicted on the Stele of Revealing as a winged disk. Heru-ra-ha is a name for Horus as the Lord of the Aeon of Thelema. Horus in his active form is known as Ra-Hoor-Khuit, seated on his throne on the Stele. In his passive form, Horus is known as Hoor-paar-kraat (Hoor-pa-kraat or Harpocrates), most often iconographically depicted in the Sign of Silence.

Yoga, Hinduism, and Buddhism

In 1902, not long before Crowley's magical mentor and tutor, Allan Bennett, moved to Burma and entered a Buddhist monastery, Crowley paid him an extended visit in Ceylon and studied under him and his guru, Ponnambalam Ramanathan.[8] Crowley thus experienced firsthand the spiritual disciplines of both Hinduism and Buddhism. Orientalists like Max Müller (1823–1900), Thomas William Rhys-

---

8 Ramanathan (1851–1930) was a Shaivite, and author of the books *On Faith or Love of God* (1897), *An Eastern Exposition of the Gospel of Jesus According to St. Matthew* (1898) and *An Eastern Exposition of the Gospel of Jesus According to St. John* (1902).

Davids (1843–1922) and Sir Edwin Arnold (1832–1904)[9] had already introduced these ideas to the West. They were embraced particularly by the Theosophical Society, which eventually migrated in both emphasis and location away from the West to Adyar, India. However, Crowley achieved an unprecedented level of integration between Eastern and Western occultism. His system of attainment goes far deeper into the techniques of yoga than any of the other Western hermetic schools.

Crowley's writings cover not only the central ideas of Buddhism and Hinduism but also place extensive emphasis on the Eight Limbs of Yoga discussed by Patanjali.[10] These include various yogic practices such as *asana* (posture) and *pranayama* (breathwork) along with many other more advanced forms of meditation and concentration.[11] Crowley refers often to the Buddhist doctrine of *dukkha* (the belief that attachment to material things is the cause of all suffering, karma, and reincarnation). The Hindu idea that our world of individuality and separateness is *maya* (illusion), and that the ultimate reality is actually universal consciousness, finds its expression in the words of Nuit in *The Book of the Law*, "the pain of division is as nothing, and the joy of dissolution all."

Holy Books of Thelema

Crowley contributed a unique body of spiritual literature to the Western esoteric tradition. These texts originated from sources beyond human understanding. Crowley taught that they should not be changed by even a single letter, lest doing so alter or erase some subtle truth in the document which we are not yet equipped to comprehend. These unchangeable documents he called "Class A," and they play the central role in the doctrine of Thelema. While *The Book of the Law* is preeminent in the Thelemic canon, several

---

9 Author of the immensely popular *Light of Asia*.

10 The Yoga Sutras of Patanjali are published in various editions. *Raja Yoga* by Vivekananda was one of Crowley's favorites. See also Crowley's *Eight Lectures on Yoga*.

11 The yogic books include "Liber E" (*asana*), "Liber Ru" (*pranayama*) and "Liber Astarté" (*bhakti yoga*). All are found in *Magick*, *The Equinox*, and *Gems from the Equinox*. Similarly, the entirety of *Book 4 Part II* (1913) is dedicated to yoga; this book is reproduced in *Magick*. An excellent modern overview is *The Weiser Concise Guide to Yoga for Magick* by Nancy Wasserman.

other Class A books followed from 1907 until the early 1920s (see table on page 66).

The "Short" (or "Tunis") "Comment" (itself a Class A document) instructs people to arrive at their own understanding of *The Book of the Law* by reading its contents and looking exclusively to Crowley's writings for clarification. Especially helpful in this regard is *The Law Is for All* (edited by Louis Wilkinson and Hymenaeus Beta). *The Law Is for All* is the "popular" edition of Crowley's voluminous commentaries, edited at Crowley's request into a concise package by his friend Louis Wilkinson (Frater T.A.K.A.T.A. [1881–1966]). Here, Crowley takes *The Book of the Law* line by line and offers his explanations and musings on its verses. *The Revival of Magick* (edited by Hymenaeus Beta and Richard Kaczynski) is also useful. It collects together the essays on Thelema and magick which Crowley wrote for a general readership, explaining himself without the technical language and references that make so many of his other books—often written for hard-core students of magick—so difficult for the beginner.

I believe it's possible to summarize some of Crowley's writings on *The Book of the Law* while remaining faithful to the intent of the "Short Comment." Key concepts he noted include the following:

Aeons: The world progresses through a series of Aeons, millennia-long epochs where the primary magical formula is based on an archetype, first of the Mother (Isis); second of the Father slain and reborn (Osiris); and then of the Child (Horus), which *The Book of the Law* heralded.

Will: The Greek word Θελημα (Thelema) or Will refers to the legitimate expression of a person's human and divine natures. It may be compared to one's purpose, function, calling, destiny, mission, or similar concept. In accordance with the principle "Do what thou wilt shall be the whole of the Law," Thelemites devote themselves entirely to the discovery and fulfillment of their true Wills. (Note: The value of Thelema (Θελημα) in the Greek Qabalah is 93, in fact, the same value as the Greek word for Love, Agapé (Αγαπη). This led Crowley to abbreviate the phrase, "Do what thou wilt shall be the whole of the Law" as "93"; and its corollary, "Love is the law, love under will" as "93 93/93." Thelemites often greet each other with "93.")

Individuality: Along with Will come other ideas which emphasize the uniqueness of every individual. Liberty and freedom are common themes in Crowley's writings, for people must be free to pursue their Wills unfettered. (See "Liber Oz," reproduced in Appendix III.) I believe this necessarily implies moral relativism—a code of conduct dictated by one's conscience rather than moral absolutes, assuming one does not interfere with the equally valid Will of others.[12] The poet and the soldier will behave differently, neither inherently wrong, yet each appropriate to the individuals' roles. On the other hand, Thelema may never be cited as an excuse for crime. This is a complex issue, perhaps best summarized by Crowley in the statement, "Collision is the only crime in the cosmos."[13]

Inclusiveness: The philosophy expounded in *Liber AL* is syncretic, which is to say it expresses ideas from Egyptian, Qabalistic, Buddhist, Christian, and other traditions. In his essay "Duty,"[14] Crowley elaborates on "Love is the law, love under will" by explaining that we ought to experience and assimilate every new point of view that we encounter, thus creating a broader foundation on which to understand the world.

On the other hand, *The Book of the Law* makes clear in no uncertain terms that its doctrine replaces those of the Old Aeon. "Behold! the rituals of the old time are black. Let the evil ones be cast away; let the good ones be purged by the prophet! Then shall this Knowledge go aright." (AL II:5). Statements such as the following from the third chapter of *The Book of the Law* also militate against the idea of a New Age multicultural approach in Thelema.

---

12 [Editor's Note: The meaning of "moral relativism" in a Thelemic context is far more complex than its typical secular humanist connotation. For the individual, morality is Absolute, "thou hast no right but to do thy will." On the other hand, what's right for you may be wrong for me. In *Magick in Theory and Practice* (page 262), Crowley described the moral teachings of Do what thou wilt as "the most sublimely austere ethical precept ever uttered, despite its apparent license..."—J.W.]

13 Crowley, Aleister. *The Law Is for All: The Authorized Popular Commentary of Liber AL vel Legis sub figura CCXX, The Book of the Law*, ed. Louis Wilkinson and Hymenaeus Beta. Tempe, AZ: New Falcon, 1991, p. 53.

14 In Crowley, Aleister, *The Revival of Magick and Other Papers*, ed. Hymenaeus Beta and Richard Kaczynski, Tempe, AZ: New Falcon, 1998.

49. I am in a secret fourfold word, the blasphemy against all gods of men.

50. Curse them! Curse them! Curse them!

51. With my Hawk's head I peck at the eyes of Jesus as he hangs upon the cross.

52. I flap my wings in the face of Mohammed & blind him.

53. With my claws I tear out the flesh of the Indian and the Buddhist, Mongol and Din.

54. Bahlasti! Ompehda! I spit on your crapulous creeds.

Joy of Union: The Theravada Buddhism with which Crowley was familiar taught that the separateness of the world is all an illusion (*maya*), ultimately leading to suffering and transmigration. By contrast, *The Book of the Law* teaches that worldly divisions, and any suffering from the illusion of separateness, are overshadowed by the spiritual ecstasy of divine, passionate union. Where Buddhism says all existence is sorrow (*dukkha*), Thelema says that existence is "pure joy."

Cast of Characters: Nuit, the Egyptian goddess of the star-filled night sky, represents infinite space, the unlimited possibilities of the universe, the All. "... I am Infinite Space, and the Infinite Stars thereof..."[15] Hadit (Had) is just one of those possibilities, a particular point embodying unique and supreme individuality, the infinite defining itself as the finite.[16] "In the sphere I am everywhere the centre, as she, the circumference, is nowhere found."[17] Ra-Hoor-Khuit is the warrior god, the child, born of the union of the All with the One, come forth in the world as sovereign manifestation. "Nu is your refuge as Hadit your light; and I am the strength, force, vigour, of your arms."[18]

---

15 *The Book of the Law*, Chapter 1, verse 22.

16 One could compare this to the "quantum cloud" idea of electrons: Unobserved, electrons exist as a probability "cloud" showing all possible locations of the electron simultaneously; once observed, this probability wave collapses and the odds of a specific location rises to 100 percent.

17 *The Book of the Law*, Chapter 2, verse 3.

18 *The Book of the Law*, Chapter 3, verse 17.

Holy Days: *The Book of the Law* outlines a calendar of Thelemic holy days. These include the rituals of the elements which Crowley mentions in the New Comment as the equinoxes and solstices (approximately March 20, June 21, September 21, and December 23). Other significant days include the anniversary of Crowley's wedding to Rose Kelly (August 12, 1903, the "feast for the first night of the Prophet and his Bride"), and the three days on which *The Book of the Law* was written (April 8, 9, and10). Three major life events are also observed for each individual: birth ("a feast for life"), puberty ("A feast for fire and a feast for water") and death ("a greater feast for death"). Finally, there are daily and nightly feasts unto Hadit and Nuit, respectively. The vernal equinox traditionally marks the beginning of the Thelemic new year, counting from 1904.

The Reception of the Holy Books

The table on page 66 briefly summarizes the names, dictation dates, and subject matter of the Class A writings, including all the Holy Books penned by Crowley. They range in length from a single page to several chapters. They may be found in *The Vision and the Voice and Other Papers*, *The Holy Books of Thelema*, and *The Equinox*.

Chronology of the Class A Writings

Title	Year written	Summary
Liber AL vel Legis	Apr. 8–10, 1904	The Book of the Law
Liber Liberi vel Lapidus Lazuli...	Oct. 30, 1907	Gives in magical language an account of the Initiation of a Master of the Temple
Liber Cordis Cincti Serpente	Oct. 30–Nov. 3, 1907	An account of the relations of the Aspirant with his Holy Guardian Angel
Liber Stellæ Rubeæ	Nov. 25, 1907	A secret ritual
Liber Arcanorum.../ Liber Carcerorum	Dec. 5–6, 14 1907, 1911	An account of the cosmic process so far as it is indicated by the Tarot Trumps
Liber Porta Lucis	Dec. 12, 1907	An account of the sending forth of the Master Therion by the A∴A∴ and an explanation of His mission.
Liber Tau vel Kabbalæ Trium Literarum	Dec. 13, 1907	A graphical interpretation of the Tarot on the plane of initiation.
Liber Trigrammaton	Dec. 14, 1907	A book of Trigrams of the Mutations of the Tao with the Yin and Yang
Liber Ararita	Winter 1907–8	Describes in magical language a very secret process of Initiation
Liber XXX Ærum vel Saecli*	1909	The Vision and the Voice
A Note upon Liber DCCCCLXIII	1910	Introduction to Liber DCCCCLXIII, ΘΕΣΑΥΡΟΥ ’ΕΙΔΩΛΩΝ, The Treasure House of Images
Liber B vel Magi	1911	An account of the Grade of Magus
Liber Tzaddi vel Hamus Hermeticus	1911	An account of Initiation
Liber Cheth vel Vallum Abiegni	1911	An account of the task of the Exempt Adept
Liber A'ash vel Capricorni Pneumatici	1911	Contains the true secret of all practical Magick
Opus Lutetiatum*	1913–1914	The Paris Working
The Short Comment	1925	To the Book of the Law

* These texts contain both Class A and Class B material.

CHAPTER SIX

Basic Mystical Exercises

Perhaps Crowley's greatest contribution to the technical practice of magick as a field of human endeavor was to inextricably link meditation and concentration to ceremonial and other forms of magick. Previous Adepts might teach and expound upon these things privately, but no one publicly stressed the importance of meditation to the extent that Crowley did. This, in fact, is one of the most important reasons his magical system works so well. It is practiced by people who have learned to focus their minds. He credited his focus on concentration and awareness practices to the influence of his two early mentors, Oscar Eckenstein and Allan Bennett.

You'll want to start a magical record. It can be a notebook or word-processing document, so long as you can record your practices and review under what circumstances you get the best results. Make notes about anything you think matters: the time of day, the weather, your mood, the positions of the planets, etc.[1] You'll forget a surprising amount of detail within hours, let alone days, after each exercise, so make your journal entries as soon as possible after you finish.

The suggested practices in this chapter are designed to help you develop daily awareness and one-pointed thought. Building upon such a foundation, your magical practices will become effective engines of your True Will. Without such a foundation, many "students of the occult" are simply fooling themselves.

"Awareness" Rituals

These rituals are designed to wake the magician out of mundane consciousness, keeping at the forefront awareness of the self and one's place in the universe, while enhancing mindfulness of the Great Work. Although Crowley never called them "awareness rituals," that is, in essence, what they are.

---

1 For examples of good magick journaling, see *Aleister Crowley and the Practice of the Magical Diary*, ed. James Wasserman.

Will (To Be Done before Meals)[2]

The first of these is the instruction on conscious eating. What better correlation than to link the body's need for food with the Aspirant's will to attain?

Using the handle of a knife, your index finger, or knuckles, tap the table three times, then five times, then another three.[3] If dining with another, this is conducted as a dialogue. If eating by yourself, you may adapt it as a monologue of simple first-person statements.

> Do what thou wilt shall be the whole of the Law.
> What is thy will?
> It is my will to eat and drink.
> To what end?
> That I may fortify my body thereby.
> To what end?
> That I may accomplish the Great Work.
> Love is the law, love under will.
> (knocking once). Fall to!

While some have criticized this practice as "like saying grace," it is also quite different. Although it shares the awareness of the sacred interaction of man and Nature, we don't ask a supreme being to bless our food. Instead, we pause in the midst of what, for many, is an automatic action (eating) to remind ourselves of *why* we're eating: That we may do the Great Work of discovering and accomplishing our True Wills. It transforms any meal into a magical, intentional act.

Solar Adorations (Liber Resh)

Another level of "awareness" ritual is "Liber Resh," in which the passage of time and diurnal journey of the Sun becomes the occasion of daily spiritual focus.

---

2 This ritual first appeared in *Moonchild* (1929), p. 79.

3 Crowley abbreviates this alarm or battery as 3-5-3. The knocks orient the consciousness to a particular magick formula, and 3-5-3 is not only 11 (the number of magick), but it also represents the union of the microcosm (5) and macrocosm (6).

"Liber Resh"[4] is an instruction to magically affirm the sun's course four times throughout the day: dawn, noon, dusk, and midnight. The practice of "Liber Resh" does one very simple thing very well: It causes the practitioner to stop whatever it is he or she may be doing and notice time's passing. And because this is done in a ritualized way, it helps the practitioner remember that whatever day-to-day routines we may have to follow to keep our daily bread on the table, there is a larger reason for this—and that reason is the Great Work.

LIBER RESH VEL HELIOS

0. These are the adorations to be performed by aspirants to the A∴A∴.

1. Let him greet the Sun at dawn, facing East, giving the sign of his grade. And let him say in a loud voice:

Hail unto Thee who art Ra in Thy rising, even unto Thee who art Ra in Thy strength, who travellest over the Heavens in Thy bark at the Uprising of the Sun.

Tahuti standeth in His splendour at the prow, and Ra-Hoor abideth at the helm.

Hail unto Thee from the Abodes of Night!

2. Also at Noon, let him greet the Sun, facing South, giving the sign of his grade. And let him say in a loud voice:

Hail unto Thee who art Ahathoor in Thy triumphing, even unto Thee who art Ahathoor in Thy beauty, who travellest over the heavens in thy bark at the Mid-course of the Sun.

Tahuti standeth in His splendour at the prow, and Ra-Hoor abideth at the helm.

Hail unto Thee from the Abodes of Morning!

3. Also, at Sunset, let him greet the Sun, facing West, giving the sign of his grade. And let him say in a loud voice:

Hail unto Thee who art Tum in Thy setting, even unto Thee who art Tum in Thy joy, who travellest over the Heavens in Thy bark at the Down-going of the Sun.

Tahuti standeth in His splendour at the prow, and Ra-Hoor abideth at the helm.

Hail unto Thee from the Abodes of Day!

---

4 The Hebrew letter ר or *resh* is assigned to the Sun in both the Qabalah and the Tarot. We present here the full text.

4. Lastly, at Midnight, let him greet the Sun, facing North, giving the sign of his grade, and let him say in a loud voice:

Hail unto thee who art Khephra in Thy hiding, even unto Thee who art Khephra in Thy silence, who travellest over the heavens in Thy bark at the Midnight Hour of the Sun.

Tahuti standeth in His splendour at the prow, and Ra-Hoor abideth at the helm.

Hail unto Thee from the Abodes of Evening.

5. And after each of these invocations thou shalt give the sign of silence, and afterward thou shalt perform the adoration that is taught thee by thy Superior. And then do thou compose Thyself to holy meditation.

6. Also it is better if in these adorations thou assume the God-form of Whom thou adorest, as if thou didst unite with Him in the adoration of That which is beyond Him.

7. Thus shalt thou ever be mindful of the Great Work which thou hast undertaken to perform, and thus shalt thou be strengthened to pursue it unto the attainment of the Stone of the Wise, the Summum Bonum, True Wisdom and Perfect Happiness.

Notes: The gods addressed at each quarter

Ra. The most common form of the sun god in Egypt is Ra. He represents the rising sun emerging new born each morning at dawn, the bringing forth of light or life from the darkness of night or death. His name is believed to derive from the verb "to create," and his cultic center was in the city of Heliopolis.

Ahathoor. The goddess Hathor, the original Egyptian mother-goddess, is often depicted as a cow. She is the consort of the Bull of Amenti, and later became a sky goddess associated with the star Sept (Sirius). She is the patron of love and sometimes called the mother of Ra (her name literally means "House of Horus"). Many of her characteristics were later subsumed by the goddess Isis.

Tum. Tum, Atum, or Atem is the primeval, self-engendered god of ancient Egypt, his name literally meaning "Completed One," i.e. one who

created himself out of the primordial watery chaos. The epithet *nefer* (good) is often attached to his name, e.g. Nefer-Tum. Later he became associated with Ra, taking on the identity of Atum-Re, the setting sun.

Khephra. This god's name comes from the Egyptian root *kheper* "to create, to transform." The root also refers to the scarab beetle. Scarabs fascinated the Egyptians because, laying their eggs in the unpromising medium of dung, they brought forth life and hence became symbols of resurrection and rebirth. The scarab beetle's habit of rolling dung into a ball in order to move it also symbolized what happened to the sun after it "perished" at dusk: the scarab god Khephra rolled it through the underworld and resurrected it back at the horizon at daybreak.

Concentration

Now that we've identified our body's required daily actions of waking, sleeping, eating, and drinking, with the Will to attain, it is time to look at actual practices designed to focus the mind even more. The best of these are contained in "Liber E vel Exercitiorum sub figura IX,"[5] of which we present some extracts below.

I

1. It is absolutely necessary that all experiments should be recorded in detail during, or immediately after, their performance.

2. It is highly important to note the physical and mental condition of the experimenter or experimenters.

3. The time and place of all experiments must be noted; also the state of the weather, and generally all conditions which might conceivably have any result upon the experiment either as adjuvants to or causes of the result, or as inhibiting it, or as sources of error.

...

5 The full text of "Liber E" is presented in *Magick, The Equinox*, and *Gems from the Equinox*.

8. The Book *John St. John* published in the first number of *The Equinox* is an example of this kind of record by a very advanced student. It is not as simply written as we could wish, but will show the method.

9. The more scientific the record is, the better. Yet the emotions should be noted, as being some of the conditions.

Let then the record be written with sincerity and care; thus with practice it will be found more and more to approximate to the ideal.

III
Asana–Posture

1. You must learn to sit perfectly still with every muscle tense for long periods.

2. You must wear no garments that interfere with the posture in any of these experiments.

3. The first position: (The God). Sit in a chair; head up, back straight, knees together, hands on knees, eyes closed.

4. The second position: (The Dragon). Kneel; buttocks resting on the heels, toes turned back, back and head straight, hands on thighs.

5. The third position: (The Ibis). Stand, hold left ankle with right hand, free forefinger on lips.

6. The fourth position: (The Thunderbolt). Sit; left heel pressing up anus, right foot poised on its toes, the heel covering the phallus; arms stretched out over the knees; head and back straight.

7. Various things will happen to you while you are practicing these positions; they must be carefully analyzed and described.

8. Note down the duration of practice; the severity of the pain (if any) which accompanies it, the degree of rigidity attained, and any other pertinent matters.

9. When you have progressed up to the point that a saucer filled to the brim with water and poised upon the head does not spill one drop during a whole hour, and when you can no longer perceive the slightest tremor in any muscle; when, in short, you are perfectly steady and easy, you will be admitted for examination; and, should you pass, you will be instructed in more complex and difficult practices.

IV
Pranayama–Regularization of the Breathing

1. At rest in one of your positions, close the right nostril with the thumb of the right hand and breathe out slowly and completely through the left nostril, while your watch marks 20 seconds. Breathe in through the same nostril for 10 seconds. Changing hands, repeat with the other nostril. Let this be continuous for one hour.

2. When this is quite easy to you, increase the periods to 30 and 15 seconds.

3. When this is quite easy to you, but not before, breathe out for 15 seconds, in for 15 seconds, and hold the breath for 15 seconds.

4. When you can do this with perfect ease and comfort for a whole hour, practice breathing out for 40 and in for 20 seconds.

5. This being attained, practice breathing out for 20, in for 10, holding the breath for 30 seconds.

6. When this has become perfectly easy to you, you may be admitted for examination, and should you pass, you will be instructed in more complex and difficult practices.

7. You will find that the presence of food in the stomach, even in small quantities, makes the practices very difficult.

8. Be very careful never to overstrain your powers; especially never get so short of breath that you are compelled to breathe out jerkily or rapidly.

9. Strive after depth, fullness, and regularity of breathing.

10. Various remarkable phenomena will very probably occur during these practices. They must be carefully analyzed and recorded.

V
Dharana–Control of Thought

1. Constrain the mind to concentrate itself upon a single simple object imagined.

The five tatwas are useful for this purpose; they are: a black oval; a blue disk; a silver crescent; a yellow square; a red triangle.

2. Proceed to combinations of simple objects; e.g. a black oval within a yellow square, and so on.

3. Proceed to simple moving objects, such as a pendulum swinging, a wheel revolving, etc. Avoid living objects.

4. Proceed to combinations of moving objects, e.g. a piston rising and falling while a pendulum is swinging. The relation between the two movements should be varied in different experiments.

Or even a system of flywheels, eccentrics, and governor.

5. During these practices the mind must be absolutely confined to the object determined upon; no other thought must be allowed to intrude upon the consciousness. The moving systems must be regular and harmonious.

6. Note carefully the duration of the experiments, the number and nature of the intruding thoughts, the tendency of the object itself to depart from the course laid out for it, and any other phenomena which may present themselves. Avoid overstrain; this is very important.

7. Proceed to imagine living objects; as a man, preferably some man known to, and respected by, yourself.

8. In the intervals of these experiments you may try to imagine the objects of the other senses, and to concentrate upon them.

For example, try to imagine the taste of chocolate, the smell of roses, the feeling of velvet, the sound of a waterfall or the ticking of a watch.

9. Endeavour finally to shut out all objects of any of the senses, and prevent all thoughts arising in your mind. When you feel you have attained some success in these practices, apply for examination, and should you pass, more complex and difficult practices will be prescribed for you.

Liber Jugorum: Control of Thought and Action[6]

One of Crowley's more controversial exercises is to have students prohibit speaking some common word ("I," "the," "but," etc.) or making some motion (such as raising the arm overhead). The inevitable infractions are punished by cutting the forearm with a razor,

---

6 "Liber III vel Jugorum" appears in *The Equinox* i.4, *Gems from the Equinox*, and *Magick*.

providing not only a deterrent but also a visible reminder and a way to count your violations.[7] The result of this exercise is a state of hyper-vigilance, reminding magicians how much of what they say or do is unconscious and thoughtless. It is important to: (a) track the number of infractions and when they happen (so you can see your improvement); and (b) remember this exercise is only for a fixed length of time: some hours, an entire day, or a week is the idea. (Crowley gave additional suggestions to those contained in "Liber III vel Jugorum" itself for the time periods in *Book IV*, Part II, Chapter 6 on the Wand.)

Here are the instructions for speech and action extracted from "Liber Jugorum":

I.

0. The Unicorn is speech. Man, rule thy Speech! How else shalt thou master the Son, and answer the Magician at the right hand gateway of the Crown?

1. Here are practices. Each may last for a week or more.

2. (a) Avoid using some common word, such as "and" or "the" or "but"; use a paraphrase.

(b) Avoid using some letter of the alphabet, such as "t", or "s", or "m"; use a paraphrase.

(c) Avoid using the pronouns and adjectives of the first person; use a paraphrase.

Of thine own ingenium devise others.

3. On each occasion that thou art betrayed into saying that thou art sworn to avoid, cut thyself sharply upon the writs or forearm with a razor; even as thou shouldst beat a disobedient dog. Feareth not the Unicorn the claws and teeth of the Lion?

4. Thine arm then serveth thee both for a warning and for a record. Thou shalt write down thy daily progress in these practices, until thou art perfectly vigilant at all times over the least word that slippeth from thy tongue.

Thus bind thyself, and thou shalt be for ever free.

---

7 Some modern students have reported good results from snapping a thick rubber band kept on the wrist.

II.

0. The Horse is Action. Man, rule thine Action. How else shalt thou master the Father, and answer the Fool at the Left Hand Gateway of the Crown?

1. Here are practices. Each may last for a week, or more.

(a) Avoiding lifting the left arm above the waist.

(b) Avoid crossing the legs.

Of thine own ingenium devise others.

2. On each occasion that thou art betrayed into doing that thou art sworn to avoid, cut thyself sharply upon the wrist or forearm with a razor; even as thou shouldst beat a disobedient dog. Feareth not the Horse the teeth of the Camel?

3. Thine arm then serveth thee both for a warning and for a record. Thou shalt write down thy daily progress in these practices, until thou art perfectly vigilant at all times over the least action that slippeth from the least of thy fingers.

Thus bind thyself, and thou shalt be for ever free.

CHAPTER SEVEN

BASIC MAGICAL EXERCISES

CLASSIC IMAGES OF THE MAGICIAN show a man wearing a long robe, wielding a stave or sword, and working in a temple with a magic circle. These trappings are indeed part of ceremonial magick, and Crowley dedicates Part 2 of *Book Four* to describing all these implements in painstaking detail. However, most of the rituals described in this chapter require no special equipment, clothing, or settings. They are designed to be read and tried without any particular preparation. If you want to jump in and get your feet wet, you can and should.

First, a caveat: Since the most important part of magick happens between your ears, anything you can do to make your work *special* will help. If you have a room—or even a closet that you can open, decorate, and face as a temple—by all means do. If you have a special piece of clothing or jewelry that you put on just for spiritual work, go right ahead. If you do any other sort of preparation— a ritual bath, lighting incense, meditating—it can only help. Just remember that these extra things aren't strictly *necessary*. Don't make these simple rituals too difficult to do every day.

Yes, every day.

Remember the adage "practice makes perfect"? Don't expect an amazing result the first time you try one of these rituals. While anything is possible, I find these rituals require a "break-in" period to get comfortable saying the words or making the gestures before anything happens.

Banishing Rituals

Banishing rituals serve several purposes. Depending on how you think magick works, you may subscribe to some or all of these: they focus the magician on the magical task at hand; they define a sacred space in which to do magick; they create a psychological barrier between this sacred space and the outside world, so you can leave mundane distractions behind during your ritual; they clean your environment of any unwanted energies, allowing you to practice scientific illuminism in an uncontaminated magical circle; they create a barrier from undesirable influences while summoning desirable spiritual/archetypal beings to guard you during your Great Work;

and they recreate the universe in miniature, so that whatever you do in your sacred space is mirrored in the larger universe according to the maxim "As above, so below."

Given all the wonderful things that banishing rituals do, they are surprisingly simple. They all involve the same basic steps (with some adding an occasional flourish):

- Centering yourself (Qabalistic Cross or similar exercise)
- Drawing a circle, setting a ward (pentagram or hexagram) at each of the four compass points, and intoning sacred words to fortify your space
- Calling guardians to the four compass points to watch over your work
- Re-centering yourself

While some traditions suggest using a consecrated dagger or wand to trace pentagrams or hexagrams, your finger (or thumb extended between clenched index and medius) and willpower are all that are needed for an effective banishing.

We'll begin with two classic rituals that Crowley borrowed from the Golden Dawn. The Lesser Banishing Ritual of the Pentagram (LBRP) uses the elemental energies of earth, air, fire, water, and spirit, while the Lesser Ritual of the Hexagram (LRH) expands your sphere of working from the terrestrial to the seven traditional planets. Nevertheless, they follow the same basic structure described earlier.

These instructions are extracted from "Liber O vel Manus et Sagittae":[1]

I

...

2. In this book it is spoken of the Sephiroth, and the Paths, of Spirits and Conjurations; of Gods, Spheres, Planes, and many other things which may or may not exist.

3. It is immaterial whether these exist or not. By doing certain things certain results will follow; students are most earnestly warned against attributing objective reality or philosophic validity to any of them.

---

1 The full text of "Liber O" appears in *Magick, The Equinox,* and *Gems from the Equinox.*

4. "The advantages to be gained from them are chiefly these:

(a) A widening of the horizon of the mind.

(b) An improvement of the control of the mind."

III

...

3. The Vibration of God-names. As a further means of identifying the human consciousness with that pure portion of it which man calls by the name of some God, let him act thus:

4. (a) Stand with arms outstretched. (See Illustration [on page 82].)

(b) Breathe in deeply through the nostrils, imagining the name of the God desired entering with the breath.

(c) Let that name descend slowly from the lungs to the heart, the solar plexus, the navel, the generative organs, and so to the feet.

(d) The moment that it appears to touch the feet, quickly advance the left foot about 12 inches, throw forward the body, and let the hands (drawn back to the side of the eyes) shoot out, so that you are standing in the typical position of the God Horus, [See Illustration] and at the same time imagine the Name as rushing up and through the body, while you breathe it out through the nostrils with the air which has been till then retained in the lungs. All this must be done with all the force of which you are capable.

(e) Then withdraw the left foot, and place the right forefinger upon the lips, so that you are in the characteristic position of the God Harpocrates. [See Illustration]

Sign of the Enterer
Horus

Sign of Silence
Harpocrates

5. It is a sign that the student is performing this correctly when a single "Vibration" entirely exhausts his physical strength. It should cause him to grow hot all over, or to perspire violently, and it should so weaken him that he will find it difficult to remain standing.

6. It is a sign of success, though only by the student himself is it perceived, when he hears the name of the God vehemently roared forth, as if by the concourse of ten thousand thunders; and it should appear to him as if that Great Voice proceeded from the Universe, and not from himself...The longer it takes for normal perception to return, the better.

IV

1. The Rituals of the Pentagram and Hexagram must be committed to memory; they are as follows:

The Lesser Ritual of the Pentagram

(i) Touching the forehead say Ateh (Unto Thee).

(ii) Touching the breast say Malkuth (The Kingdom).

(iii) Touching the right shoulder, say ve-Geburah (and the Power).

(iv) Touching the left shoulder, say ve-Gedulah (and the Glory).

(v) Clasping the hands upon the breast, say le-Olahm, Amen (To the Ages, Amen).

(vi) Turning to the East make a pentagram (that of Earth) with the proper weapon (usually the Wand). Say (i.e. vibrate) I H V H.

(vii) Turning to the South, the same, but say A D N I.

(viii) Turning to the West, the same, but say A H I H.

(ix) Turning to the North, the same, but say A G L A.

Pronounce: Ye-ho-wau, Adonai, Eheieh, Agla.

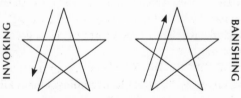

THE PENTAGRAMS OF EARTH

(x) Extending the arms in the form of a Cross say:

(xi) Before me Raphael;

(xii) Behind me Gabriel;

(xiii) On my right hand Michael.

(xiv) On my left hand Auriel;

(xv) For about me flames the Pentagram,

(xvi) And in the Column stands the six-rayed Star.

(xvii–xxi) Repeat (i) to (v), the Qabalistic Cross.

The Lesser Ritual of the Hexagram

This ritual is to be performed after the Lesser Ritual of the Pentagram.

(i) Stand upright, feet together, left arm at side, right across body, holding the wand or other weapon upright in the median line. Then face East and say:

(ii) I.N.R.I.

Yod. Nun. Resh. Yod.

Virgo, Isis, Mighty Mother.

Scorpio, Apophis, Destroyer.

Sol, Osiris, Slain and Risen.

Isis, Apophis, Osiris, IAO.

(iii) Extend the arms in the form of a cross, and say: "The Sign of Osiris Slain." (See Illustration.)

(iv) Raise the right arm to point upwards, keeping the elbow square, and lower the left arm to point downwards, keeping the elbow square, while turning the head over the left shoulder looking down so that the eyes follow the left forearm, and say, "The Sign of the Mourning of Isis." (See Illustration).

(v) Raise the arms at an angle of sixty degrees to each other above the head, which is thrown back, and say, "The Sign of Apophis and Typhon." (See Illustration.)

(vi) Cross the arms on the breast, and bow the head and say, "The Sign of Osiris Risen." (See Illustration.)

(vii) Extend the arms again as in (iii) and cross them again as in (vi) saying: "L.V.X., Lux, the Light of the Cross".

(viii) With the magical weapon trace the Hexagram of Fire in the East, saying,

Ararita (אראריתא). This Word consists of the initials of a sentence which means "One is His Beginning: One is His Individuality: His Permutation is One."

THE SIGNS OF THE GRADES

1. Earth: the god Set fighting.
2. Air: the god Shu supporting the sky.
3. Water: the goddess Auramoth
4. Fire: the goddess Thoum-aesh-neith
5–6. Spirit: the rending and closing of the veil.

7–10. THE LVX SIGNS.

7. + Osiris slain — the Cross.
8. L Isis mourning — the Svastika
9. V Typhon — the Trident
10. X Osiris risen — the Pentagram

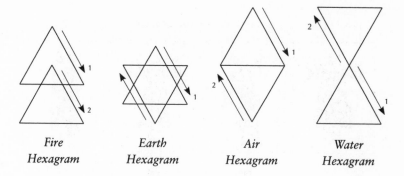

| Fire Hexagram | Earth Hexagram | Air Hexagram | Water Hexagram |

This hexagram consists of two equilateral triangles, both apices pointed upwards. Begin at the top of the upper triangle and trace it in a dextro-rotary direction. The top of the lower triangle should coincide with the central point of the upper triangle.

Trace the Hexagram of Earth in the South, saying "ARARITA." This Hexagram has the apex of the lower triangle pointing downwards, and it should be capable of inscription in a circle.

Trace the Hexagram of Air in the West, saying "ARARITA." This Hexagram is like that of Earth; but the bases of the triangles coincide, forming a diamond.

(xi) Trace the hexagram of Water in the North, saying "ARARITA." This hexagram has the lower triangle placed above the upper, so that their apices coincide.

(xii) Repeat (i–vii).

The Banishing Ritual is identical, save that the direction of the Hexagrams must be reversed.

...

2. These rituals should be practiced until the figures drawn appear in flame, in flame so near to physical flame that it would perhaps be visible to the eyes of a bystander, were one present. It is alleged that some persons have attained the power of actually kindling fire by these means. Whether this be so or not, the power is not one to be aimed at.

3. Success in "banishing" is known by a "feeling of cleanliness" in the atmosphere; success in "invoking" by a "feeling of holiness." It is unfortunate that these terms are so vague.

But at least make sure of this: that any imaginary figure or being shall instantly obey the will of the student, when he uses the appropriate figure. In obstinate cases, the form of the appropriate God may be assumed.

4. The banishing rituals should be used at the commencement of any ceremony whatever. Next, the student should use a general invocation, such as the "Preliminary Invocation" in the *Goetia* as well as a special invocation to suit the nature of his working.

5. Success in these verbal invocations is so subtle a matter, and its grades so delicately shaded, that it must be left to the good sense of the student to decide whether or not he should be satisfied with his result.

The Star Ruby[2]

Crowley created a version of the LBRP that specifically invokes the Thelemic current and improves these basic formulae. It begins with a gesture of exorcism, a concise statement of the ritual's purpose. At the beginning, the magician exclaims "*Apo pantos kakodaimonos!*" which is Greek for "Away every evil spirit!" This is followed by the revised Qabalistic Cross, an invocation/consecration pronounced *Soi O Phallé, Iscuros, Eucharistos, IAO.* In keeping with Crowley's idea that clockwise motion is for invoking and counterclockwise is for banishing, the circle is drawn *counterclockwise.* ΘHPION, roared in the east, is pronounced *Therion.*

Similarly, the summoning of the four guardians is also in Greek: "*Pro mou Iunges, opiso mou Teletarchai, epi dexia Synocheis, eparistera Daimones, phlegei gar peri mou ho Aster ton Pente, kai en tei stelei ho Aster ton Hex esteke.*" ["Before me the Iynges, behind me the Teletarchs, on my right hand the Synoches, on my left the Dæmons, for about me flame the Star of Five and in the pillar stands the Star of Six."] The names of these guardians come from *The Chaldean Oracles,* an ancient Greek text of magic

---

2 The first version of this ritual appeared in *The Book of Lies.* Subsequent versions, such as that given here from *Magick,* changed some of the names.

and theurgy that was very popular in the Golden Dawn and with Crowley.

LIBER XXV
THE STAR RUBY

Facing East, in the centre, draw deep deep deep thy breath closing thy mouth with thy right forefinger prest against thy lower lip. Then dashing down the hand with a great sweep back and out, expelling forcibly thy breath, cry ΑΠΟ ΠΑΝΤΟΣ ΚΑΚΟΔΑΙΜΟΝΟΣ.

With the same forefinger touch thy forehead, and say ΣΟΙ, thy member, and say Ω ΦΑΛΛΕ,* thy right shoulder, and say ΙΣΧΥΡΟΣ, thy left shoulder, and say ΕΥΧΑΡΙΣΤΟΣ; then clasp thine hands, locking the fingers, and cry ΙΑΩ. Advance to the East. Imagine strongly a Pentagram, aright, in thy forehead. Drawing the hands to the eyes, fling it forth, making the sign of Horus and roar ΘΗΡΙΟΝ. Retire thine hand in the sign of Hoor-paar-Kraat.

Go round to the North and repeat; but say NUIT.

Go round to the West and repeat; but whisper BABALON.

Go round to the South and repeat; but bellow HADIT.

Completing the circle widdershins, retire to the centre and raise thy voice in the Paian, with these words ΙΩ ΠΑΝ, with the signs of N.O.X.

Extend the arms in the form of a Tau and say low but clear:

ΠΡΟ ΜΟΥ ΙΥΓΓΕΣ

ΟΠΙΣΩ ΜΟΥ ΤΕΛΕΤΑΡΧΑΙ

ΕΠΙ ΔΕΞΙΑ ΣΥΝΟΧΕΙΣ

ΕΠΑΡΙΣΤΕΡΑ ΔΑΙΜΟΝΕΣ

ΦΛΕΓΕΙ ΓΑΡ ΠΕΡΙ ΜΟΥ Ο ΑΣΤΗΡ ΤΩΝ ΠΕΝΤΕ

ΚΑΙ ΕΝ ΤΗΙ ΣΤΗΛΗΙ Ω ΑΣΤΗΡ ΤΩΝ ΕΞ ΕΣΤΗΧΕ.

Repeat the Cross Qabalistic, as above, and end as thou didst begin.

[* The secret sense of these words is to be sought in the numeration thereof. —A.C.]

The NOX Signs

Puer
(Boy, 6°=5□)

Vir
(Strength, 7°=4□)

Puella
(Girl, Babe
of the Abyss)

Mulier
(Woman, Babe
of the Abyss)

Mater Triumphans
(Triumphant Mother,
8°=3□)

CHAPTER EIGHT

SEX MAGICK

CROWLEY'S SCIENTIFIC EXPLORATION of magick—seeking that which works and is reproducible—predictably led him to sex. Having grown up in a strict fundamentalist household in Victorian England, Crowley was a vocal critic of the contradictions and social ills surrounding sexual repression.

> Mankind must learn that the sexual instinct is in its true nature ennobling. The shocking evils which we all deplore are principally due to the perversion produced by suppressions. The feeling that it is shameful and the sense of sin cause concealment—which is ignoble—and internal conflict, which creates distortion, neurosis, and ends in explosion ... *The Book of the Law* solves the sexual problem completely. Each individual has an absolute right to satisfy his sexual instinct as is physiologically proper for him. The one injunction is to treat all such acts as sacraments.[1]

In Thelema, the individual's liberty to fulfill his Will extends to sex. Crowley applied the energy of this most powerful and most circumcribed human instinct to the practice of magick and the performance of the Great Work. He discusses sex magick throughout his writings, almost always in veiled language. Whether you read *Liber Aleph*, *The Book of Thoth*, or *The Book of Lies*, the hints are there, hidden in plain sight. Sometimes the metaphor is easy to see: "Thou art tossed about in the grip of the storm for an æon and an æon and an æon. But thou givest not thy sap; thou fallest not."[2] Sometimes it is not. Indeed, one of Crowley's most misunderstood passages falls into this category. In chapter 12 of *Magick in Theory and Practice* ("Of the Bloody Sacrifice: And Matters Cognate"), we read: "It appears from the Magical Records of Frater Perdurabo that He made this particular sacrifice [i.e., "a male child of perfect innocence and high intelligence"] on an average about 150 times

---

1 *Confessions*, p. 851.

2 "Liber A'ash vel Capricorni Pneumatici sub figura CCCLXX" v.5. This Class A text can be found in *The Equinox*, *Gems from the Equinox*, *Holy Books of Thelema*, and *Magick*.

every year between 1912 E.V. and 1928 E.V." In Crowley's veiled word play (which has caused us no end of trouble since!), this "sacrifice" refers to ejaculation (without conception). Perhaps his least-veiled description occurs in "Energized Enthusiasm."[3]

How Crowley incorporated sex into his magical practice changed over time. I would suggest that between 1909 and 1912, he used sex as transgression, as stimulus, or as part of a larger ritual. However, when Theodor Reuss explained the secret of the O.T.O.'s Sovereign Sanctuary, Crowley's practice shifted toward sex itself as the magical act. This change is well worth examining.

Sex as Transgression

Breaking religious taboos about sex is a spiritually potent and transformative practice that encompasses traditions from Hindu Tantra to Jewish Frankism. Shattering social taboos can be just as empowering. In 1909, while trekking through the Algerian desert and working through the 30 Enochian Calls,[4] Crowley's visions were interrupted by a spiritual barrier: he had worked the 30th through 15th Calls, but with the 14th he encountered only dark veils and a voice instructing him to depart. Realizing that an offering of some kind was in order, but having no suitable offering so far in the desert, Crowley offered himself upon a makeshift altar as a sexual sacrifice to his scribe and student, Victor Neuburg.[5] It is worth noting that this was not his first homosexual encounter. However, in a ritual context, it served as a ceremonial rejection of the social and religious values of his time. He had an epiphany, and as a result the barrier to the 14th and subsequent Calls was removed.

In instances like this, it would be easy to dismiss him as a pervert or hedonist. However, an observation by his student and friend Gerald Yorke (1901–1983) bears repeating: "Crowley didn't *enjoy* his perversions! He performed them to overcome his horror

---

3 Found in *The Equinox* and *Gems from the Equinox*.

4 A series of invocations left from the angelic magical work of Dr. John Dee and Edward Kelly. See page 55.

5 *Perdurabo*, p. 158–9; *The Equinox* 1(10):114–5.

of them."[6] In other words, the magical power came from breaking a taboo, not from feeding a kink.[7]

Sex as Stimulus

The use of sex as a stimulus for ecstatic trance states is a technique that Crowley stumbled upon by accident—meeting the wizard Ab-ul-diz in the process. In a state of sex- and alcohol-induced exhaustion, his lover, Mary Desti, went into a trance and became a conduit whereby the præterhuman intelligence Ab-ul-diz could communicate a message to Crowley: He was to find (or write) a magical text called *Book Four* (see page 30). It was not unlike Rose Crowley "channeling" Aiwass seven years before that resulted in the reception of *The Book of the Law*.[8] Nor was it the last time this would happen to him. Similar channelings occurred during the Amalantrah Working (January through June, 1918), and even as late as 1933 with the Scarlet Woman Pearl Brooksmith. In view of Crowley's carefully cultivated skepticism and insistence on testing the legitimacy of psychic experience, in each instance he required quite a bit of convincing before accepting such communication as a genuine magical phenomenon.

Sex as an Element in Ritual

For a ceremonial magician, the most obvious form of sex magick is to include sex as part of a ritual: as a way to raise and release energy/intention/will. Crowley's writings provide many examples, the best, perhaps, being from *The Book of Lies*, The Star Sapphire.[9]

---

6 Fuller, *The Magical Dilemma of Victor Neuburg*, p. 244.

7 For a full exploration of Crowley's use of sacred transgression, see my "Taboo and Transformation in the Works of Aleister Crowley" in Hyatt, Christopher (ed.), *Rebels and Devils*, 2nd ed., Tempe, Ariz: New Falcon, 2000, p. 171–9.

8 Crowley never speaks of Rose's trance state as occurring in conjunction with sex; furthermore, her trance state lasted longer than the duration of the evening; Rose, it seemed, could contact Aiwass at will. Nevertheless, being on their honeymoon, it's not unreasonable to admit that sex could have been involved.

9 "The Star Sapphire" appears in *The Book of Lies*, *Magick*, and *Gems from the Equinox*.

It largely follows the same structure as the pentagram and hexagram rituals presented in Chapter 7:

LIBER XXXVI
THE STAR SAPPHIRE

Let the Adept be armed with his Magick Rood [and provided with his mystic rose].

In the centre, let him give the L.V.X. signs; or if he know them, if he will and dare do them, and can keep silent about them, the signs of N.O.X. being the signs of Puer, Vir, Puella, Mulier. Omit the sign. I.R.

Then let him advance to the East and make the Holy Hexagram, saying: *Pater et Mater unus deus Ararita.*

Let him go round to the South, make the Holy Hexagram and say: *Mater et Filius unus deus Ararita.*

Let him go round to the North, make the Holy Hexagram and then say: *Filia et Pater unus deus Ararita.*

Let him then return to the Centre, and so to The Centre of All (making the Rosy Cross as he may know how) saying *Ararita Ararita Ararita*

(In this the Signs shall be those of Set Triumphant and of Baphomet. Also shall Set appear in the Circle. Let him drink of the Sacrament and let him communicate the same.) Then let him say: *Omnia in Duos: Duo in Unum: Unus in Nihil: Haec nec Quatuor nec Omnia nec Duo nec Unus nec Nihil Sunt.*

Gloria Patri et Matri et Filio et Filiae et Spiritui Sancto externo et Spiritui Sancto interno ut erat est erit in saecula Saeculorum sex in uno per nomen Septem in uno Ararita.

Let him then repeat the signs of L.V.X. but not the signs of N.O.X.: for it is not he that shall arise in the Sign of Isis Rejoicing.

The Latin words mean "Father and Mother are the one God ARARITA," "Mother and Son are the one God ARARITA," "Son and Daughter are the one God ARARITA" and "Daughter and Father are the one God ARARITA." Note how the second person in the sentence becomes the first one in the following sentence: "Pater et Mater" becomes "Mater et Filius," then "Filius et Filia," and finally "Filia et Pater." These four personages express the Tetragrammaton formula, given by the Hebrew name of God (YHVH), whose letters (from right to left) correspond to the Father, Mother, Son, and Daughter. ARARITA is an anagram of the Hebrew sentence meaning "One is His Beginning; One is His Individuality; His Permutation is One." The remaining Latin means "All in Two; Two in One; One in None; These are neither Four nor All nor Two nor One nor None," and "Glory be to the Father and the Mother and the Son and the Daughter and the Holy Spirit without and the Holy Spirit within as it was, is, will be for ages and ages, six in one through the name seven in one ARARITA."

Herewith is Crowley's commentary on the Star Sapphire from *The Book of Lies:*

> The Star Sapphire corresponds with the Star-Ruby of Chapter 25 [See chapter 6 of this book—Ed.]; 36 being the square of 6, as 25 is of 5.
>
> This chapter gives the real and perfect Ritual of the Hexagram.
>
> It would be improper to comment further upon an official ritual of the A∴A∴.

Summary

Although Crowley used veiled language—and occasionally even puns—to describe his approach to sacred sexuality, he was absolutely serious. Anyone who says sex magick is easy hasn't tried it: the rituals involve preparation, study, discipline, and practice. Crowley's exploration of this once taboo topic has electrified the imagination of later generations, making him, according to Ohio State University's Hugh Urban,[10] one of the main figures responsible for defining Western Tantra.

10 Urban, Hugh. *Magia Sexualis: Sex, Magic, and Liberation in Modern Western Esotericism.* Berkeley: University of California Press, 2006.

"The Great Symbol of Solomon"
from Lévi's Dogma and Ritual of High Magic (1861).

ONE STAR IN SIGHT.

...

[Opening poem omitted.]

A glimpse of the structure and system of the
Great White Brotherhood.

A∴A∴ *

Do what thou wilt shall be the whole of the Law.

1. The Order of the Star called S.S. is, in respect of its existence upon the Earth, an organized body of men and women distinguished among their fellows by the qualities here enumerated. They exist in their own Truth, which is both universal and unique. They move in accordance with their own Wills, which are each unique, yet coherent with the universal will.

2. The order consists of eleven grades or degrees, and is numbered as follows: these compose three groups, the Orders of the S.S., of the R.C., and of the G.D. respectively.

The Order of the S.S.

Ipsissimus	$10° = 1°$
Magus	$9° = 2°$
Magister Templi	$8° = 3°$

The Order of the R.C.
(Babe of the Abyss—the link)

Adeptus Exemptus	$7° = 4°$
Adeptus Major	$6° = 5°$
Adeptus Minor	$5° = 6°$

---

* The Name of the Order and those of its three divisions are not disclosed to the profane. Certain swindlers have recently stolen the initials A∴A∴ in order to profit by its reputation. [Footnotes in Appendix I are by A.C.]

The Order of the G.D.
(Dominus Liminis—the link)

Philosophus	$4° = 7°$
Practicus	$3° = 8°$
Zelator	$2° = 9°$
Neophyte	$1° = 10°$
Probationer	$0° = 0°$

(These figures have special meanings to the initiated and are commonly employed to designate the grades.)

The general characteristics and attributions of these Grades are indicated by their correspondences on the Tree of Life, as may be studied in detail in the Book 777.

Student.—His business is to acquire a general intellectual knowledge of all systems of attainment, as declared in the prescribed books. (See curriculum in Appendix I [of *Book IV*, Part 3].)

Probationer.—His principal business is to begin such practices as he my prefer, and to write a careful record of the same for one year.

Neophyte.—Has to acquire perfect control of the Astral Plane.

Zelator.—His main work is to achieve complete success in Asana and Pranayama. He also begins to study the formula of the Rosy Cross.

Practicus.—Is expected to complete his intellectual training, and in particular to study the Qabalah.

Philosophus.—Is expected to complete his moral training. He is tested in Devotion to the Order.

Dominus Liminis.—Is expected to show mastery of Pratyahara and Dharana.

Adeptus (without).—Is expected to perform the Great Work and to attain the Knowledge and Conversation of the Holy Guardian Angel.

Adeptus (within).—Is admitted to the practice of the formula of the Rosy Cross on entering the College of the Holy Ghost.

Adeptus (Major).—Obtains a general mastery of practical Magick, though without comprehension.

Adeptus (Exemptus).—Completes in perfection all these matters. He then either (*a*) becomes a Brother of the Left Hand Path or, (*b*) is stripped of all his attainments and of himself as well, even of his Holy Guardian Angel, and becomes a Babe of the Abyss, who, having transcended the Reason, does nothing but grow in the womb of its mother. It then finds itself a

Magister Templi.—(Master of the Temple): whose functions are fully described in Liber 418, as is this whole initiation from Adeptus Exemptus. See also "Aha!". His principal business is to tend his "garden" of disciples, and to obtain a perfect understanding of the Universe. He is a Master of Samadhi.

Magus.—Attains to wisdom, declares his law (See Liber I, vel Magi) and is a Master of all Magick in its greatest and highest sense.

Ipsissimus.—Is beyond all this and beyond all comprehension of those of lower degrees.

But of these last three Grades see some further account in *The Temple of Solomon the King, Equinox* I to X and elsewhere.

It should be stated that these Grades are not necessarily attained fully, and in strict consecution, or manifested wholly on all planes. The subject is very difficult, and entirely beyond the limits of this small treatise.

We append a more detailed account.

3. *The Order of the S.S.* is composed of those who have crossed the Abyss; the implications of this expression may be studied in Liber 418, the 14th, 13th, 12th, 11th, 10th, and 9th Aethyrs in particular.

All members of the Order are in full possession of the Formulae of Attainment, both mystical or inwardly-directed and Magical or outwardly-directed. They have full experience of attainment in both these paths.

They are all, however, bound by the original and fundamental Oath of the Order, to devote their energy to assisting the Progress of their Inferiors in the Order. Those who accept the rewards of their emancipation for themselves are no longer within the Order.

Members of the Order are each entitled to found Orders dependent on themselves on the lines of the R. C. and G. D. orders, to cover types of emancipation and illumination not contemplated by the original (or main) system. All such orders must, however, be constituted in harmony with the A∴A∴ as regards the essential principles.

All members of the Order are in possession of the Word of the existing Aeon, and govern themselves thereby.

They are entitled to communicate directly with any and every member of the Order, as they may deem fitting.

Every active Member of the Order has destroyed all that He is and all that he has on crossing the Abyss; but a star is cast forth in the Heavens to enlighten the Earth, so that he may possess a vehicle wherein he may communicate with mankind. The quality and position of this star, and its functions, are determined by the nature of the incarnations transcended by him.

4. The Grade of Ipsissimus is not to be described fully; but its opening is indicated in *Liber I vel Magi.*

There is also an account in a certain secret document to be published when propriety permits. Here it is only said this: The Ipsissimus is wholly free from all limitations soever, existing in the nature of all things without discriminations of quantity or quality between them. He has identified Being and not-Being and Becoming, action and non-action and tendency to action, with all other such triplicities, not distinguishing between them in respect of any conditions, or between any one thing and any other thing as to whether it is with or without conditions.

He is sworn to accept this Grade in the presence of a witness, and to express its nature in word and deed, but to withdraw Himself at once within the veils of his natural manifestation as a man, and to keep silence during his human life as to the fact of his attainment, even to the other members of the Order.

The Ipsissimus is pre-eminently the Master of all modes of existence; that is, his being is entirely free from internal or external necessity. His work is to destroy all tendencies to construct or to cancel such necessities. He is the Master of the Law of Unsubstantiality (Anatta).

The Ipsissimus has no relation as such with any Being: He has no will in any direction, and no Consciousness of any kind involving duality, for in Him all is accomplished; as it is written "beyond the Word and the Fool, yea, beyond the Word and the Fool."

5. The Grade of Magus is described in Liber I vel Magi, and there are accounts of its character in Liber 418 in the Higher Aethyrs.

There is also a full and precise description of the attainment of this Grade in the Magical Record of the Beast 666.

The essential characteristic of the Grade is that its possessor utters a Creative Magical Word, which transforms the planet on which he lives by the installation of new officers to preside over its initiation. This can take place only at an "Equinox of the Gods" at the end of an

"Aeon"; that is, when the secret formula which expresses the Law of its action becomes outworn and useless to its further development.

(Thus "Suckling" is the formula of an infant: when teeth appear it marks a new "Aeon", whose "Word" is "Eating").

A Magus can therefore only appear as such to the world at intervals of some centuries; accounts of historical Magi, and their Words, are given in *Liber Aleph*.

This does not mean that only one man can attain this Grade in any one Aeon, so far as the Order is concerned. A man can make personal progress equivalent to that of a "Word of an Aeon"; but he will identify himself with the current word, and exert his will to establish it, lest he conflict with the work of the Magus who uttered the Word of the Aeon in which He is living.

The Magus is pre-eminently the Master of Magick, that is, his will is entirely free from internal diversion or external opposition; His work is to create a new Universe in accordance with His Will. He is the Master of the Law of Change (Anicca).

To attain the Grade of Ipsissimus he must accomplish three tasks, destroying the Three Guardians mentioned in Liber 418, the 3rd Aethyr; Madness, and Falsehood, and Glamour, that is, Duality in Act, Word and Thought.

6. The Grade of Master of the Temple is described in Liber 418 as above indicated. There are full accounts in the Magical Diaries of the Beast 666, who was cast forth into the Heaven of Jupiter, and of Omnia in Uno, Unus in Omnibus, who was cast forth into the sphere of the Elements.

The essential Attainment is the perfect annihilation of that personality which limits and oppresses his true self.

The Magister Templi is pre-eminently the Master of Mysticism, that is, His Understanding is entirely free from internal contradiction or external obscurity; His word is to comprehend the existing Universe in accordance with His own Mind. He is the Master of the Law of Sorrow (Dukkha).

To attain the grade of Magus he must accomplish Three Tasks; the renunciation of His enjoyment of the Infinite so that he may formulate Himself as the Finite; the acquisition of the practical secrets alike of initiating and governing His proposed new Universe and the identification of himself with the impersonal idea of Love. Any neophyte of the Order (or, as some say, any person soever) possesses the right to claim the Grade of Master of the Temple by taking the Oath of the Grade. It is hardly necessary to observe that to do so is the most sublime and awful responsibility which it is possible to assume, and an unworthy person who does so incurs the most terrific penalties by his presumption.

7. *The Order of the R.C.* The Grade of the Babe of the Abyss is not a Grade in the proper sense, being rather a passage between the two Orders. Its characteristics are wholly negative, as it is attained by the resolve of the Adeptus Exemptus to surrender all that he has and is for ever. It is an annihilation of all the bonds that compose the self or constitute the Cosmos, a resolution of all complexities into their elements, and these thereby cease to manifest, since things are only knowable in respect of their relation to, and reaction on, other things.

8. The Grade of Adeptus Exemptus confers authority to govern the two lower Orders of R.C. and G.D.

The Adept must prepare and publish a thesis setting forth His knowledge of the Universe, and his proposals for its welfare and progress. He will thus be known as the leader of a school of thought.

(Éliphas Lévi's *Clef des Grands Mysteres,* the works of Swedenborg, von Eckartshausen, Robert Fludd, Paracelsus, Newton, Bolyai, Hinton, Berkeley, Loyola, etc., etc., are examples of such essays.)

He will have attained all but the supreme summits of meditation, and should be already prepared to perceive that the only possible course for him is to devote himself utterly to helping his fellow creatures.

To attain the Grade of Magister Templi, he must perform two tasks; the emancipation from thought by putting each idea against its opposite, and refusing to prefer either; and the consecration of himself as a pure vehicle for the influence of the order to which he aspires.

He must then decide upon the critical adventure of our Order; the absolute abandonment of himself and his attainments. He cannot remain indefinitely an Exempt Adept; he is pushed onward by the irresistible momentum that he has generated.

Should he fail, by will or weakness, to make his self-annihilation absolute, he is none the less thrust forth into the Abyss; but instead of being received and reconstructed in the Third Order, as a Babe in the womb of our Lady BABALON, under the Night of Pan, to grow up to be Himself wholly and truly as He was not previously, he remains in the Abyss, secreting his elements round his Ego as if isolated from the

Universe, and becomes what is called a "Black Brother." Such a being is gradually disintegrated from lack of nourishment and the slow but certain action of the attraction of the rest of the Universe, despite efforts to insulate and protect himself, and to aggrandize himself by predatory practices. He may indeed prosper for a while, but in the end he must perish, especially when with a new Aeon a new word is proclaimed which he cannot and will not hear, so that he is handicapped by trying to use an obsolete method of Magick, like a man with a boomerang in a battle where every one else has a rifle.

9. The Grade of Adeptus Major confers Magical Powers (strictly so-called) of the second rank.

His work is to use these to support the authority of the Exempt Adept his superior. (This is not to be understood as an obligation of personal subservience or even loyalty; but as a necessary part of his duty to assist his inferiors. For the authority of the Teaching and governing Adept is the basis of all orderly work.)

To attain the Grade of Adeptus Exemptus, he must accomplish Three Tasks; the acquisition of absolute Self-Reliance, working in complete isolation, yet transmitting the word of his superior clearly, forcibly and subtly; and the comprehension and use of the Revolution of the wheel of force, under its three successive forms of Radiation, Conduction and Convection (Mercury, Sulphur, Salt; or Sattvas, Rajas, Tamas), with their corresponding natures on other planes. Thirdly, he must exert his whole power and authority to govern the Members of lower Grades with balanced vigour and initiative in such a way as to allow no dispute or complaint; he must employ to this end the formula called "The Beast conjoined with the Woman" which establishes a new incarnation of deity; as in the legends of Leda, Semele, Miriam, Pasiphae, and others. He must set up this ideal for the orders which he rules, so that they may possess a not too abstract rallying point suited to their undeveloped states.

10. The Grade of Adeptus Minor is the main theme of the instructions of the A∴A∴. It is characterized by the Attainment of the Knowledge and Conversation of the Holy Guardian Angel. (See *The Equinox, The Temple of Solomon the King; The Vision and the Voice* 8th Aethyr; also Liber Samekh, etc., etc.) This is the essential work of every man; none other ranks with it either for personal progress or for power to help one's fellows. This unachieved, man is no more than the unhappiest and blindest of animals. He is conscious of his own incomprehensible calamity, and clumsily incapable of repairing

it. Achieved, he is no less than the co-heir of gods, a Lord of Light. He is conscious of his own consecrated course, and confidently ready to run it. The Adeptus Minor needs little help or guidance even from his superiors in our Order.

His work is to manifest the Beauty of the Order to the world, in the way that his superiors enjoin, and his genius dictates.

To attain the Grade Adeptus Major, he must accomplish two tasks; the equilibration of himself, especially as to his passions, so that he has no preference for any one course of conduct over another, and the fulfilment of every action by its complement, so that whatever he does leaves him without temptation to wander from the way of his True Will.

Secondly, he must keep silence, while he nails his body to the tree of his creative will, in the shape of that Will, leaving his head and arms to form the symbol of Light, as if to make oath that his every thought, word and deed should express the Light derived from the God with which he has identified his life, his love and his liberty— symbolized by his heart, his phallus, and his legs. It is impossible to lay down precise rules by which a man may attain to the knowledge and conversation of His Holy Guardian Angel; for that is the particular secret of each one of us; a secret not to be told or even divined by any other, whatever his grade. It is the Holy of Holies, whereof each man is his own High Priest, and none knoweth the Name of his brother's God, or the Rite that invokes Him.

The Masters of the A∴A∴ have therefore made no attempt to institute any regular ritual for this central Work of their Order, save the generalised instructions in Liber 418 (the 8th Aethyr) and the detailed Canon and Rubric of the Mass actually used with success by FRATER PERDURABO in His attainment. This has been written down by Himself in Liber Samekh. But they have published such accounts as those in *The Temple of Solomon the King* and in *John St. John*. They have taken the only proper course; to train aspirants to this attainment in the theory and practice of the whole of Magick and Mysticism, so that each man may be expert in the handling of all known weapons, and free to choose and to use those which his own experience and instinct dictate as proper when he essays the Great Experiment.

He is furthermore trained to the one habit essential to Membership of the A∴A∴; he must regard all his attainments as primarily the property of those less advanced aspirants who are confided to his charge.

No attainment soever is officially recognised by the A∴A∴ unless the immediate inferior of the person in question has been fitted by him to take his place.

The rule is not rigidly applied in all cases, as it would lead to congestion, especially in the lower grades where the need is greatest, and the conditions most confused; but it is never relaxed in the Order of the R.C. or of the S.S.: save only in One Case.

There is also a rule that the Members of the A∴A∴ shall not know each other officially, save only each Member his superior who introduced him and his inferior whom he has himself introduced.

This rule has been relaxed, and a "Grand Neophyte" appointed to superintend all Members of the Order of the G.D. The real object of the rule was to prevent Members of the same Grade working together and so blurring each other's individuality; also to prevent work developing into social intercourse.

The Grades of the Order of the G.D. are fully described in Liber 185,* and there is no need to amplify what is there stated. It must however, be carefully remarked that in each of these preliminary Grades there are appointed certain tasks appropriate, and that the ample accomplishment of each and every one of these is insisted upon with the most rigorous rigidity.†

Members of the A∴A∴ of whatever grade are not bound or expected or even encouraged to work on any stated lines, or with any special object, save as has been above set forth. There is however an absolute prohibition to accept money or other material reward, directly or indirectly, in respect of any service connected with the Order, for personal profit or advantage. The penalty is immediate expulsion, with no possibility of reinstatement on any terms soever.

But all members must of necessity work in accordance with the facts of Nature, just as an architect must allow of the Law of Gravitation, or a sailor reckon with currents.

---

* This book is published in the Equinox Vol. III No. 2. [Not issued during Crowley's lifetime. "Liber 185" has since been published in *The Vision and the Voice and Other Papers* (*The Equinox* Vol. IV No. 1).]

† Liber 185 need not be quoted at length. It is needful only to say that the Aspirant is trained systematically and comprehensively in the various technical practices which form the basis of Our Work. One may become expert in any or all of these without necessarily making any real progress, just as a man might be first-rate at grammar, syntax, and prosody without being able to write a single line of good poetry, although the greatest poet in soul is unable to express himself without the aid of those three elements of literary composition.

So must all Members of the A∴A∴ work by the Magical Formula of the Aeon.

They must accept the Book of the Law as the Word and the Letter of Truth, and the sole Rule of Life.[*]

They must acknowledge the Authority of the Beast 666 and of the Scarlet Woman as in the book it is defined, and accept Their Will[†] as concentrating the Will of our Whole Order. They must accept the Crowned and Conquering Child as the Lord of the Aeon, and exert themselves to establish His reign upon Earth. They must acknowledge that "The word of the Law is ΘΕΛΗΜΑ" and that "Love is the law, love under will."

Each member must make it his main work to discover for himself his own true will, and to do it, and do nothing else.[‡]

He must accept those orders in the Book of the Law that apply to himself as being necessarily in accordance with his own true will, and execute the same to the letter with all the energy, courage, and ability that he can command. This applies especially to the work of extending the Law in the world, wherein his proof is his own success, the witness of his Life to the Law that hath given him light in his ways, and liberty to pursue them. Thus doing, he payeth his debt to the Law that hath freed him by working its will to free all men; and he proveth himself a true man in our Order by willing to bring his fellows into freedom.

By thus ordering his disposition, he will fit himself in the best possible manner for the task of understanding and mastering the divers technical methods prescribed by the A∴A∴ for Mystical and Magical attainment.

He will thus prepare himself properly for the crisis of his career in the Order, the attainment of the Knowledge and Conversation of his Holy Guardian Angel.

---

[*] This is not in contradiction with the absolute right of every person to do his own true Will. But any True Will is of necessity in harmony with the facts of Existence; and to refuse to accept the Book of the Law is to create a conflict within Nature, as if a physicist insisted on using an incorrect formula of mechanics as the basis of an experiment.

[†] "Their Will"—not, of course, their wishes as individual human beings, but their will as officers of the New Aeon.

[‡] It is not considered "essential to right conduct" to be an active propagandist of the Law, and so on; it may, or may not, be the True Will of any particular person to do so. But since the fundamental purpose of the Order is to further the Attainment of humanity, membership implies, by definition, the Will to help mankind by the means best adapted thereto.

His Angel shall lead him anon to the summit of the Order of the R.C. and make him ready to face the unspeakable terror of the Abyss which lies between Manhood and Godhead; teach him to Know that agony, to Dare that destiny, to Will that catastrophe, and to keep Silence for ever as he accomplishes the act of annihilation.

From the Abyss comes No Man forth, but a Star startles the Earth, and our Order rejoices above that Abyss that the Beast hath begotten one more Babe in the Womb of Our Lady, His concubine, the Scarlet Woman, BABALON.

There is not need to instruct a Babe thus born, for in the Abyss it was purified of every poison of personality; its ascent to the highest is assured, in its season, and it hath no need of seasons for it is conscious that all conditions are no more than forms of its fancy.

Such is a brief account, adapted as far as may be to the average aspirant to Adeptship, or Attainment, or Initiation, or Mastership, or Union with God, or Spiritual Development, or Mahatmaship, or Freedom, or Occult Knowledge, or whatever he may call his inmost need of Truth, of our Order of A∴A∴.

It is designed principally to awake interest in the possibilities of human progress, and to proclaim the principles of the A∴A∴.

The outline given of the several successive steps is exact; the two crises—the Angel and the Abyss—are necessary features in every career. The other tasks are not always accomplished in the order given here; one man, for example, may acquire many of the qualities peculiar to the Adeptus Major, and yet lack some of those proper to the Practicus.* But the system here given shows the correct order of events, as they are arranged in Nature; and in no case is it safe for a

---

* The natural talents of individuals differ very widely. The late Sir Richard Jebb, one of the greatest classical scholars of modern times, was so inferior to the average mediocrity in mathematics, that despite repeated efforts he could not pass the "little go" at Cambridge—which the dullest minds can usually do. He was so deeply esteemed for his classics that a special "Grace" was placeted so as to admit him to matriculation. Similarly a brilliant Exorcist might be an incompetent Diviner. In such a case the A∴A∴ would refuse to swerve from Its system; the Aspirant would be compelled to remain at the Barrier until he succeeded in breaking it down, though a new incarnation were necessary to permit him to do so. But no technical failure of any kind soever could necessarily prevent him from accomplishing the Two Critical Tasks, since the fact of his incarnation itself proves that he has taken the Oath which entitled him to attain to the Knowledge and Conversation of his Holy Guardian Angel, and the annihilation of this Ego. One might therefore be an Adeptus Minor or even a Magister Templi, in essence, though refused official recognition by the A∴A∴ as a Zelator owing to (say) a nervous defect which prevented him from acquiring a Posture which was "steady and easy" as required by the Task of that grade.

man to neglect to master any single detail, however dreary and distasteful it may seem. It often does so, indeed; that only insists on the necessity of dealing with it. The dislike and contempt for it bear witness to a weakness and incompleteness in the nature which disowns it; that particular gap in one's defenses may admit the enemy at the very turning-point of some battle. Worse, one were shamed for ever if one's inferior should happen to ask for advice and aid on that subject and one were to fail in service to him! His failure—one's own failure also! No step, however well won for oneself, till he is ready for his own advance!

Every Member of the A∴A∴ must be armed at all points, and expert with every weapon. The examinations in every Grade are strict and severe; no loose or vague answers are accepted. In intellectual questions, the candidate must display no less mastery of his subject than if he were entered in the "final" for Doctor of Science or Law at a first-class University.

In examination of physical practices, there is a standardized test. In Asana, for instance, the candidate must remain motionless for a given time, his success being gauged by poising on his head a cup filled with water to the brim; if he spill one drop, he is rejected.

He is tested in "the Spirit Vision" or "Astral Journeying" by giving him a symbol unknown and unintelligible to him, and he must interpret its nature by means of a vision as exactly as if he had read its name and description in the book when it was chosen.

The power to make and "charge" talismans is tested as if they were scientific instruments of precision, as they are.

In the Qabalah, the candidate must discover for himself, and prove to the examiner beyond all doubt, the properties of a number never previously examined by any student.

In invocation the divine force must be made as manifest and unmistakable as the effects of chloroform; in evocation, the spirit called forth must be at least as visible and tangible as the heaviest vapors; in divination, the answer must be as precise as a scientific thesis, and as accurate as an audit; in meditation, the results must read like a specialist's report of a classical case.

By such methods, the A∴A∴ intends to make occult science as systematic and scientific as chemistry; to rescue it from the ill repute which, thanks both to the ignorant and dishonest quacks that have prostituted its name, and to the fanatical and narrow-minded enthusiasts that have turned it into a fetish, has made it an object of aversion to those very minds whose enthusiasm and integrity make them most in need of its benefits, and most fit to obtain them.

It is the one really important science, for it transcends the conditions of material existence and so is not liable to perish with the planet, and it must be studied as a science, sceptically, with the utmost energy and patience.

The A∴A∴ possesses the secrets of success; it makes no secret of its knowledge, and if its secrets are not everywhere known and practiced, it is because the abuses connected with the name of occult science disincline official investigators to examine the evidence at their disposal.

This paper has been written not only with the object of attracting individual seekers into the way of Truth, but of affirming the propriety of the methods of the A∴A∴ as the basis for the next great step in the advance of human knowledge.

Love is the law, love under will.

O. M. 7°= 4□ A∴A∴
Praemonstrator of the
Order of the R... C...

Given from the Collegium ad Spiritum Sanctum, Cefalù, Sicily, in the Seventeenth Year of the Aeon of Horus, the Sun being in 23° ♍ and the Moon in 14° ♓.

LIBER CI

ORDO TEMPLI ORIENTIS
AN OPEN LETTER TO THOSE WHO MAY WISH TO JOIN THE ORDER

...

[Long salutation omitted.]

Do what thou wilt shall be the whole of the Law.

IT HAS BEEN REPRESENTED TO US that some persons who are worthy to join the O.T.O. consider the fees and subscriptions rather high. This is due to your failure to explain properly the great advantages offered by the Order. We desire you therefore presently to note, and to cause to be circulated throughout the Order, and among those of the profane who may seem worthy to join it, these matters following concerning the duties and the privileges of members of the earlier degrees of the O.T.O. as regards material affairs. And for convenience we shall classify these as pertaining to the Twelve Houses of the Heaven, but also by numbered clauses for the sake of such as understand not the so-called Science of the Stars. First, therefore, concerning the duties of the Brethren. Yet with our Order every duty is also a privilege, so that it is impossible wholly to separate them.

OF THE DUTIES OF THE BRETHREN

FIRST HOUSE

1. There is no law beyond Do what thou wilt. Yet it is well for Brethren to study daily in the Volume of the Sacred Law, *Liber Legis*, for therein is much counsel concerning this, how best they may carry out this will.

SECOND HOUSE

2. The private purse of every Brother should always be at the disposal of any Brother who may be in need. But in such a case it is a great mischief if the one ask, and the other consent; for if the former be really in need, his pride is wounded by his asking; and if not, the door is opened to beggars and imposters, and all manner of arrant knaves and rogues such as are no true Brethren. But the Brother

who is possessed of this world's goods should make it his business to watch the necessity of all those Brethren with whom he may be personally acquainted, anticipating their wants in so wise and kindly and delicate a manner that it shall appear as if it were the payment of a debt. And what help is given shall be given with discretion, so that the relief may be permanent rather than temporary.

3. All Brethren shall be exceedingly punctual in the payment of Lodge Dues. This is to take precedence of all other calls upon the purse.

THIRD HOUSE

4. The Brethren shall be diligent in preaching the Law of Thelema. In all writings they shall be careful to use the prescribed greetings; likewise in speech, even with strangers.

5. They shall respond heartily to every summons of the Lodge or Chapter to which they may belong, not lightly making excuse.

6. Brethren should use every opportunity of assisting each other in their tastes, businesses, or professions, whether by direct dealing with Brethren in preference to others, or by speaking well of them, or as may suggest itself. It seems desirable, when possible, that where two or more Brethren of the same Lodge are engaged in the same work, they should seek to amalgamate the same by entering into partnership. Thus in time great and powerful corporations may arise from small individual enterprises.

7. They shall be diligent in circulating all tracts, manifestos, and all other communications which the Order may from time to time give out for the instruction or emancipation of the profane.

8. They may offer suitable books and pictures to the Libraries of the Profess-Houses of the Order.

FOURTH HOUSE

9. Every Brother who may possess mines, land, or houses more than he can himself constantly occupy, should donate part of such mines or land, or one or more of such houses to the Order.

10. Property thus given will be administered if he desire it in his own interest, thus effecting a saving, since large estates are more economically handled than small. But the Order will use such property as may happen to lie idle for the moment in such ways as it may seem good, lending an unlet house (for example) to some Brother who is in need, or allowing an unused hall to be occupied by a Lodge.

11. (Yet in view of the great objects of the Order, endowment is welcome.)

12. Every Brother shall show himself solicitous of the comfort and happiness of any Brother who may be old, attending not only to all material wants, but to his amusement, so that his declining years may be made joyful.

FIFTH HOUSE

13. Every Brother shall seek constantly to give pleasure to all Brethren with whom he is acquainted, whether by entertainment or conversation, or in any other manner that may suggest itself. It will frequently and naturally arise that love itself springs up between members of the Order, for that they have so many and sacred interests in common. Such love is peculiarly holy, and is to be encouraged.

14. All children of Brethren are to be considered as children of the whole Order, and to be protected and aided in every way by its members severally, as by its organization collectively. No distinction is to be made with regard to the conditions surrounding the birth of any child.

15. There is an especially sacred duty, which every Brother should fulfil, with regard to all children, those born without the Order included. This duty is to instruct them in the Law of Thelema, to teach them independence and freedom of thought and character, and to warn them that servility and cowardice are the most deadly diseases of the human soul.

SIXTH HOUSE

16. Personal or domestic attendants should be chosen from among the members of the Order when possible, and great tact and courtesy are to be employed in dealing with them.

17. They, on their part, will render willing and intelligent service.

18. While in Lodge, and on special occasions, they are to be treated as Brothers, with perfect equality; such behavior is undesirable during the hours of service, and familiarity, subversive as it is of all discipline and order, is to be avoided by adopting a complete and marked change of manner and address.

19. This applies to all persons in subordinate positions, but not to the Brethren Servient in the Profess-Houses of the Order, who, giving service without recompense, are to be honored as hosts.

20. In case of the sickness of any Brother, it is the duty of all Brethren who know him personally to attend him, to see that he want for nothing, and to report if necessary his needs to the Lodge, or to Grand Lodge itself.

21. Those Brethren who happen to be doctors or nurses will naturally give their skill and care with even more than their customary joy in service.

22. All Brethren are bound by their fealty to offer their service in their particular trade, business, or profession, to the Grand Lodge. For example, a stationer will supply Grand Lodge with paper, vellum, and the like; a bookseller offer any books to the Library of Grand Lodge which the Librarian may desire to possess; a lawyer will execute any legal business for Grand Lodge, and a railway or steamship owner or director see to it that the Great Officers travel in comfort wherever they may wish to go.

23. Visitors from other Lodges are to be accorded the treatment of ambassadors; this will apply most especially to Sovereign Grand Inspector Generals of the Order on their tours of inspection. All hospitality and courtesy shown to such is shown to Ourselves, not to them only.

Seventh House

24. It is desirable that the marriage partner of any Brother should also be a member of the Order. Neglect to insist upon this leads frequently to serious trouble for both parties, especially the uninitiate.

25. Lawsuits between members of the Order are absolutely forbidden, on pain of immediate expulsion and loss of all privileges, even of those accumulated by past good conduct referred to in the second part of this instruction.

26. All disputes between Brethren should be referred firstly to the Master or Masters of their Lodge or Lodges in conference; if a composition be not arrived at in this manner, the dispute is to be referred to the Grand Tribunal, which will arbitrate thereon, and its decision is to be accepted as final.

27. Refusal to apply for or accept such decision shall entail expulsion from the Order, and the other party is then at liberty to seek his redress in the Courts of Profane Justice.

28. Members of the Order are to regard those without its pale as possessing no rights of any kind, since they have not accepted the Law, and are therefore, as it were, troglodytes, survivals of a past civilization, and to be treated accordingly. Kindness should be shown

towards them, as towards any other animal, and every effort should be made to bring them into Freedom.

29. Any injury done by any person without the Order to any person within it may be brought before the Grand Tribunal, which will, if it deem right and fit, use all its power to redress or to avenge it.

30. In the case of any Brother being accused of an offence against the criminal law of the country in which he resides, so that any other Brother cognizant of the fact feels bound in self-defense to bring accusation, he shall report the matter to the Grand Tribunal as well as to the Civil Authority, claiming exemption on this ground.

31. The accused Brother will, however, be defended by the Order to the utmost of its power on his affirming his innocence upon the Volume of the Sacred Law in the Ordeal appointed ad hoc by the Grand Tribunal itself.

32. Public enemies of the country of any Brother shall be treated as such while in the field, and slain or captured as the officer of the Brother may command. But within the precincts of the Lodge all such divisions are to be forgotten absolutely; and as children of One Father the enemies of the hour before and the hour after are to dwell in peace, amity, and fraternity.

Eighth House

33. Every Brother is expected to bear witness in his last will and testament to the great benefit that he hath received from the Order by bestowing upon it part or the whole of his goods, as he may deem fit.

34. The death of a Brother is not to be an occasion of melancholy, but of rejoicing; the Brethren of his Lodge shall gather together and make a banquet with music and dancing and all manner of gladness. It is of the greatest importance that this shall be done, for thereby the inherited fear of death which is deep-seated as instinct in us will gradually be rooted out. It is a legacy from the dead aeon of Osiris, and it is our duty to kill it in ourselves that our children and our children's children may be born free from the curse.

Ninth House

35. Every Brother is expected to spend a great part of his spare time in the study of the principles of the Law and of the Order, and in searching out the key to its great and manifold mysteries.

36. He should also do all in his power to spread the Law, especially taking long journeys, when possible, to remote places, there to sow the seed of the Law.

Tenth House

37. All pregnant women are especially sacred to members of the Order, and no effort should be spared to bring them to acceptance of the Law of Freedom, so that the unborn may benefit by that impression. They should be induced to become members of the Order, so that the child may be born under its aegis.

38. If the mother that is to be have asserted her will to be so in contempt and defiance of the Tabus of the slave-gods, she is to be regarded as especially suitable to our Order, and the Master of the Lodge in her district shall offer to become, as it were, godfather to the child, who shall be trained specially, if the mother so wishes, as a servant of the Order, in one of its Profess-Houses.

39. Special Profess-Houses for the care of women of the Order, or those whose husbands or lovers are members of the Order, will be instituted, so that the frontal duty of womankind may be carried out in all comfort and honour.

40. Every Brother is expected to use all his influence with persons in a superior station of life (so called) to induce them to join the Order. Royal personages, ministers of State, high officials in the Diplomatic, Naval, Military, and Civil Services are particularly to be sought after, for it is intended ultimately that the temporal power of the State be brought into the Law, and led into freedom and prosperity by the application of its principles.

41. Colleges of the Order will presently be established where the children of its members may be trained in all trades, businesses, and professions, and there they may study the liberal arts and humane letters, as well as our holy and arcane science. Brethren are expected to do all in their power to make possible the establishment of such Universities.

Eleventh House

42. Every Brother is expected to do all in his power to induce his personal friends to accept the Law and join the Order. He should therefore endeavor to make new friends outside the Order, for the purpose of widening its scope.

TWELFTH HOUSE

43. The Brethren are bound to secrecy only with regard to the nature of the rituals of our Order, and to our words, signs, etc. The general principles of the Order may be fully explained, so far as they are understood below the VI°; as it is written, "The ordeals I write not: the rituals shall be half known and half concealed: the Law is for all." It is to be observed that punctual performance of these duties, so that the report thereof is noised abroad and the fame of it cometh even unto the Throne of the Supreme and Holy King himself, will weigh heavily in the scale when it comes to be a question of the high advancement of a Brother in the Order.

OF THE PRIVILEGES OF THE BRETHREN

FIRST HOUSE

44. The first and greatest of all privileges of a Brother is to be a Brother; to have accepted the Law, to have become free and independent, to have destroyed all fear, whether of custom, or of faith, or of other men, or of death itself. In other papers the joy and glory of those who have accepted The Book of the Law as the sole rule of life is largely, though never fully, explained; and we will not here recapitulate the same.

SECOND HOUSE

45. All Brethren who may fall into indigence have a right to the direct assistance of the Order up to the full amount of fees and subscriptions paid by them up to the time of application. This will be regarded as a loan, but no interest will be charged upon it. That this privilege may not be abused, the Grand Tribunal will decide whether or no such application is made in good faith.

THIRD HOUSE

46. Members of the Order will be permitted to use the Library in any of our Profess-Houses.

47. Circulating Libraries will presently be established.

48. Brethren who may be traveling have a right to the hospitality of the Master of the Lodge of the district for a period of three days.

FOURTH HOUSE

49. Brethren of all grades may be invited to sojourn in the Profess-Houses of the Order by Grand Lodge; and such invitation may confidently be expected as the reward of merit. There they will be able to make the personal acquaintance of members of the higher Grades, learn of the deeper workings of the Order, obtain the benefit of personal instruction, and in all ways fit themselves for advancement.

50. Brethren of advanced years and known merit who desire to follow the religious life may be asked to reside permanently in such houses.

51. In the higher degrees Brethren have the right to reside in our Profess-Houses for a portion of every year, as shown:

VI°. Two weeks.	VII°. Two months.
G.T. One month.	S.G.C. Three months.
P.R.S. Six weeks.	VIII°. Six months.

52. Members of the IX°, who share among themselves the whole property of the Order according to the rules of that degree, may, of course, reside there permanently. Indeed, the house of every Brother of this grade is, ipso facto, a Profess-House of the Order.

FIFTH HOUSE

53. All Brethren may expect the warmest co-operation in their pleasures and amusements from other members of the Order. The perfect freedom and security afforded by the Law allows the characters of all Brethren to expand to the very limits of their nature, and the great joy and gladness with which they are constantly overflowing make them the best of companions. "They shall rejoice, our chosen; who sorroweth is not of us. Beauty and strength, leaping laughter and delicious languor, force and fire, are of us."

54. Children of all Brethren are entitled to the care of the Order, and arrangements will be made to educate them in certain of the Profess-Houses of the Order.

55. Children of Brethren who are left orphans will be officially adopted by the Master of his Lodge, or if the latter decline, by the Supreme Holy King himself, and treated in all ways as if they were his own.

56. Brethren who have a right to some especial interest in any child whose mother is not a member of the Order may recommend it especially to the care of their lodges or of Grand Lodge.

SIXTH HOUSE

57. In sickness all Brethren have the right to medical or surgical care and attendance from any Brethren of the Lodge who may be physicians, surgeons, or nurses.

58. In special necessity the Supreme Holy King will send his own attendants.

59. Where circumstances warrant it, in cases of lives of great value to the Order and the like, he may even permit the administration of that secret Medicine which is known to members of the IX°.

60. Members of the Order may expect Brethren to busy themselves in finding remunerative occupation for them, where they lack it, or, if possible, to employ them personally.

SEVENTH HOUSE

61. Members of the Order may expect to find suitable marriage partners in the extremely select body to which they belong. Community of interest and hope being already established, it is natural to suppose that where mutual attraction also exists, a marriage will result in perfect happiness. (There are special considerations in this matter which apply to the VII° and cannot be discussed in this place.)

62. As explained above, Brethren are entirely free of most legal burdens, since lawsuits are not permitted within the Order, and since they may call upon the legal advisers of the Order to defend them against their enemies in case of need.

EIGHTH HOUSE

63. All Brethren are entitled after death to the proper disposal of their remains according to the rites of the Order and their grade in it.

64. If the Brother so desire, the entire amount of the fees and subscriptions which he has paid during his life will be handed over by the Order to his heirs and legatees. The Order thus affords an absolute system of insurance in addition to its other benefits.

NINTH HOUSE

65. The Order teaches the only perfect and satisfactory system of philosophy, religion, and science, leading its members step by step to knowledge and power hardly even dreamed of by the profane.

66. Brethren of the Order who take long journeys overseas are received in places where they sojourn at the Profess-Houses of the Order for the period of one month.

TENTH HOUSE

67. Women of the Order who are about to become mothers receive all care, attention, and honor from all Brethren.

68. Special Profess-Houses will be established for their convenience, should they wish to take advantage of them.

69. The Order offers great social advantages to its members, bringing them as it does into constant association with men and women of high rank.

70. The Order offers extraordinary opportunities to its members in their trades, businesses, or professions, aiding them by cooperation, and securing them clients or customers.

ELEVENTH HOUSE

71. The Order offers friendship to its members, bringing together men and women of similar character, taste, and aspiration.

TWELFTH HOUSE

72. The secrecy of the Order provides it members with an inviolable shroud of concealment.

73. The crime of slander, which causes so great a proportion of human misery, is rendered extremely dangerous, if not impossible, within the Order by a clause in the Obligation of the Third Degree.

74. The Order exercises its whole power to relieve its members of any constraint to which they may be subjected, attacking with vigor any person or persons who may endeavor to subject them to compulsion, and in all other ways aiding in the complete emancipation of the Brethren from aught that may seek to restrain them from doing That Which They Will.

It is to be observed that these privileges being so vast, it is incumbent upon the honour of every Brother not to abuse them, and the sponsors of any Brother who does so, as well as he himself, will be held strictly to account by the Grand Tribunal. The utmost frankness and good faith between Brethren is essential to the easy and harmonious working of our system, and the Executive Power will see to it that these are encouraged by all means possible, and that breach of them is swiftly and silently suppressed.

Love is the law, love under will.

Our fatherly benediction, and the Blessing of the All-Father in the Outer and the Inner be upon you.

BAPHOMET X° O.T.O., IRELAND, IONA, AND ALL THE BRITAINS

LIBER LXXVII

Oz: "the law of
the strong:
this is our law
and the joy
of the world."
— *AL. II. 21*

"Do what thou wilt shall be the whole of the Law."
— *AL. I. 40*

"thou has no right but to do thy will. Do that, and no
other shall say nay." — *AL. I. 42–3*

"Every man and every woman is a star." — *AL. I. 3*

There is no god but man.

1. Man has the right to live by his own law —
   to live in the way that he wills to do:
   to work as he will:
   to play as he will:
   to rest as he will:
   to die when and how he will.

2. Man has the right to eat what he will:
   to drink what he will:
   to dwell where he will:
   to move as he will on the face of the earth.

3. Man has the right to think what he will:
   to speak what he will:
   to write what he will:
   to draw, paint, carve, etch, mould, build as he will:
   to dress as he will.

4. Man has the right to love as he will: —
   "take your fill and will of love as ye will,
   when, where and with whom ye will." — *AL. I. 51*

5. Man has the right to kill those who would thwart
   these rights.

"the slaves shall serve." — *AL. II. 58*

"Love is the law, love under will." — *AL. I. 57*

Aleister Crowley

Appendix IV

Contact Information

The following organizations are points of contact for more information regarding O.T.O., A∴A∴, and E.G.C. Readers are recommended to check the organization's Web site for current contact information and to locate a group near you.

Ordo Templi Orientis

International Headquarters

Web site:	*http://www.oto.org*
Mailing address:	Secretary General, Frater Aion
	P.O. Box 33 20 12
	D-14180 Berlin, Germany
Email address:	sg@oto.org

United States

Web site:	
Grand Lodge:	*http://www.oto-usa.org*
Local bodies:	*http://www.oto-usa.org/bodies.html*
Mailing address:	Grand Secretary General
	Ordo Templi Orientis U.S.A.
	P.O. Box 2313
	Maple Grove, MN 55311
Email address:	gsg@oto-usa.org

United Kingdom

Web site:	
Grand Lodge:	*http://www.oto-uk.org*
Local bodies:	*http://www.oto-uk.org/OTO-contact.php*
Mailing address:	BM Thelema
	London WC1N 3XX
Email address:	gsg@oto-uk.org

Australia

Web site:	
Grand Lodge:	*http://www.otoaustralia.org.au*
Local bodies:	*http://www.otoaustralia.org.au/main.htm*
Mailing address:	Australian Grand Lodge, OTO
	P.O. Box 576
	Waverly NSW 2024
Email address:	gsg@otoaustralia.org.au

Ecclesia Gnostica Catholica

If your area is not listed, contact your nearest O.T.O. body (see above) for more information.

United States
Web site: *http://www.oto-usa.org/egc.html*
Email address: egc@oto-usa.org

United Kingdom
Web site: *http://www.oto-uk.org/EGC-home.php*
Mailing address: EGC Secretary
                       c/o BM Thelema
                       London WC1N 3XX
                       England
Email address: egc@oto-uk.org

A∴A∴

Web site: *http://www.outercol.org*
Mailing address: Chancellor
                       BM ANKH
                       London WC1N 3XX
                       England

Other Online Resources

http://lib.oto-usa.org
The online library of the Unites States Grand Lodge of O.T.O. contains some of Crowley's key texts in electronic format.

http://www.hermetic.com/sabazius
The Invisible Basilica of Sabazius (the Primate of the E.G.C. in America) contains a superb collection of essays on many topics related to Ecclesia Gnostica Catholica.

http://www.gnosticmass.org
Includes a downloadable PDF Mass Missal suitable for printing in booklet forms, as well as a performance commentary by Bishops TAHUTI and MARA.

BIBLIOGRAPHY

Crowley works (in alphabetical order)

777 vel Prolegomena Symbolica ad Systemam Sceptico-Mysticæ Viæ Explicande, Fundamentum Hieroglyphicum Sanctissimorum Scientiæ Summæ. London: Walter Scott, 1909.

777 and Other Qabalistic Writings. York Beach, ME: Samuel Weiser, 1973.

Aleister Crowley and the Practice of the Magical Diary, rev. and exp., ed. James Wasserman. San Francisco: Weiser Books, 2006.

Book 4, Part 1. Frater Perdurabo & Soror Virakam. [Aleister Crowley and Mary Desti]. London: Weiland & Co., 1912–1913.

Book 4, Part 2. Frater Perdurabo & Soror Virakam. [Aleister Crowley and Mary Desti]. London: Weiland & Co., 1913.

The Book of Lies: Which is also Falsely Called Breaks. The Wanderings or Falsifications of the One Thought of Frater Perdurabo, which Thought is in Itself Untrue. Frater Perdurabo. [pseud.] London: Weiland & Co., 1913.

The Book of the Goetia of Solomon the King, Translated into the English Tongue by a Dead Hand and Adorned with Diverse Other Matters Germane, Delightful to the Wise, the Whole Edited, Verified, Introduced and Commented by Aleister Crowley, trans. S. L. Mathers, ed. Aleister Crowley. Inverness: Society for the Propagation of Religious Truth, 1904. [*The Goetia: The Lesser Key of Solomon the King: Lemegeton— Clavicla Salomonis Regis, Book One*, illustrated second edition with new annotations and illustrations by Aleister Crowley, ed. Hymenaeus Beta. York Beach, ME: Samuel Weiser, 1995.]

The Book of the Law. See *Liber AL vel Legis.*

The Book of Thoth: A Short Essay on the Tarot of the Egyptians. The Master Therion [pseud.] London: O.T.O., 1944.

"A Brief Abstract Representation of the Universe Derived by Doctor John Dee through the Skrying of Sir Edward Kelly." *The Equinox* 1912 1(7):229–243; 1(8):99–128.

"(On) A Burmese river." *Vanity Fair* 1901, 3 February, 135; 10 February, 169; 17 February, 201; 24 February, 232; 3 March, 269; 31 March, 393.

The Confessions of Aleister Crowley, ed. John Symonds and Kenneth Grant. London: Jonathan Cape, 1969. See also *The Spirit of Solitude.*

Crowley on Drugs: Essays, Diaries and Poetry concerning Drugs, Magick, Mysticism and Consciousness, ed. Hymenaeus Beta and Richard Kaczynski. Forthcoming.

The Diary of a Drug Fiend. London: William Collins & Sons., 1922.

"The drug panic." A London Physician [pseud.] *The English Review* 1922, July, 65–70.

"Duty." In, Crowley, Aleister. *The Revival of Magick and Other Papers*, ed. Hymenaeus Beta and Richard Kaczynski. Tempe, AZ: New Falcon, 1988.

"Ecclesiæ Gnosticæ Catholicæ Canon Missæ." *The International* 1918, 12(3):70–4. Reprinted in *The Equinox* 1919 3(1): 247–70; and later in *Magick in Theory and Practice*, 179–82.

Eight Lectures on Yoga. Mahatma Guru Sri Paramahansa Shivaji. [pseud.] London: O.T.O., 1939.

"Elder Eel." *The Equinox* 1912 1(8):215–29.

"Energized Enthusiasm: A Note on Theurgy." *The Equinox* 1913 1(9):17–46.

The Equinox, 1(1-10). 1909–1913. London.

The Equinox 3(10). Ed. Hymenaeus Beta. New York: Thelema Publications, 1986.

Gems from the Equinox: Instructions for Aleister Crowley for His Own Magical Order, ed. Israel Regardie. San Francisco: Weiser Books, 2007.

The Gnostic Mass (Liber XV). See *Ecclesiæ Gnosticæ Catholicæ Canon Missæ.*

"The great drug delusion." A New York Specialist [pseud.] *The English Review* 1922, June, 571–6.

The Holy Books of Thelema, ed. Hymenaeus Beta. York Beach, ME: Samuel Weiser, 1983.

The Law is for All: The Authorized Popular Commentary on Liber AL vel Legis sub figura CCXX The Book of the Law, ed. Louis Wilkinson and Hymenaeus Beta. Tempe, AZ: New Falcon, 1996.

"Liber A vel Armorum sub figura CCCXII." *The Equinox* 1910 1(4): 15–9.

"Liber A'ash vel Capricorni Pneumatici sub figura CCCLXX." *The Equinox* 1911, 1(6):33–9.

Liber AL vel Legis. First published as "Liber L vel Legis," *The Equinox*, 1913 1(10):11–33. Edition with short comment first published London: O.T.O., 1938.

Liber Aleph vel CXI: The Book of Wisdom or Folly in the Form of an Epistle of 666 The Great Wild Beast to his Son 777. West Point, CA: Thelema Publishing Co., 1961.

"Liber Ararita." See *Holy Books of Thelema*, pp. 215–29.

"Liber Arcanorum των Atu του Tahuti quas Vidit Asar in Amenti sub figura CCXXXI/Liber Carcerorum των Qliphoth cuv Suis Geniis Adduntur Sigilla et Nomina Eorum." *The Equinox* 1912 1(7):69–74.

"Liber Astarté vel Liber Berylli sub figura CLXXV." *The Equinox* 1912, 1(7):37–58.

"Liber B vel Magi sub figura I." *The Equinox* 1911, 1(7):5–9.

"Liber Cheth vel Vallum Abiegni sub figura CLVI." *The Equinox* 1911, 1(6):23–7.

Liber Collegii Sancti sub figura CLXXXV. London: privately printed, 1910. Reprinted in *Gems from the Equinox*.

"Liber Cordis Cincti Serpente." *The Equinox* 1919, 3(1):63–98.

"Liber CXCIV: An Intimation with Reference to the Constitution of the Order." *The Equinox* 1919, 3(1):239–46.

"Liber E vel Exercitiorum sub figura IX." *The Equinox* 1909, 1(7):23–34.

"Liber III vel Jugorum." *The Equinox* 1910 1(4):9–14.

"Liber Liberi vel Lapidus Lazuli, Adumbratio Kabbalæ Ægyptiorum sub figura VII." See *Holy Books of Thelema*, p. 7–35.

"Liber Libræ, the Book of the Balance." *The Equinox* 1909, 1(1): 15–21.

"Liber O vel Manus et Sagittæ sub figura VI." *The Equinox* 1909, 1(2): 11–30.

"Liber Porta Lucis sub figura X." *The Equinox* 1911, 1(6):3–7.

"Liber Resh vel Helios sub figura CC." *The Equinox* 1911, 1(6):29–32.

"Liber RV vel Spiritus sub figura CCVI." *The Equinox* 1912, 1(7):59–67.

"Liber Samekh: Theurgia Goetia Summa Congressus Cum Dæmone sub Figura DCCC." See *Magick in Theory and Practice*, pp. 265–301.

"Liber Stellæ Rubeæ." *The Equinox* 1912, 1(7):29–36.

"Liber Tau vel Kabbalæ Trium Literarum sub figura CD." *The Equinox* 1912, 1(7):75–7.

"Liber Trigrammaton sub figura XXVII." See *The Holy Books of Thelema*, pp. 43–9.

"Liber Tzaddi vel Hamus Hermeticus sub figura XC." *The Equinox* 1911, 1(6):17–22.

"Liber XIII vel Graduum Montis Abiegni: A Syllabus of the Steps upon the Path." *The Equinox* 1910, 1(3):3–8.

"Liber XVI vel Causæ." *The Equinox* 1919, 3(1):53–61.

"Liber XXX Ærum vel Sæculi sub figura CCCCXVIII: (Being of the Angels of the 30 Æthyrs): The Vision and the Voice." *The Equinox* 1911, 1(5), special supplement.

"Liber ΘΕΣΑΥΡΟΥ 'ΕΙΔΩΛΩΝ sub figura DCCCCLXIII: The Treasure-House of Images." *The Equinox* 1910, 1(3), special supplement.

Little Essays toward Truth. London: O.T.O., 1938.

Magick: Liber ABA, Book 4 part I–IV. Crowley, Aleister with Mary Desti and Leila Waddell. Edited, annotated and introduced by Hymenaeus Beta. 2nd rev. ed. York Beach, ME: Samuel Weiser, 1997.

Magick in Theory and Practice. The Master Therion [pseud.] Paris: Lecram Press, 1929.

Magick without Tears, ed. Israel Regardie. St. Paul, MN: Llewellyn, 1973.

Moonchild: A Prologue. London: Mandrake Press, 1929.

Olla: An Anthology of Song. London: O.T.O., 1946.

"One Star in Sight." In *Magick in Theory and Practice*, pp. 229–44.

Opus Lutetiatum/The Paris Working. See *The Vision and the Voice with Commentary and Other Papers*, pp. 343–409.

The Revival of Magick and Other Essays, ed. Hymenaeus Beta and Richard Kaczynski. Tempe, AZ: New Falcon, 1998.

"The Rites of Eleusis." *The Equinox* 1911, 1(6), special supplement.

Seven Lithographs By Clot from the Water-Colours of Auguste Rodin with a Chaplet of Verse By Aleister Crowley. London: Chiswick Press, 1907.

"The Short Comment." See *Liber AL vel Legis.*

The Spirit of Solitude: An Autohagiography. Subsequently Re-Antichristened The Confessions of Aleister Crowley. London: Mandrake Press, 1929. [Abridged ed., *The Confessions of Aleister Crowley*, ed. John Symonds and Kenneth Grant. London: Jonathan Cape, 1969.]

"The Star Ruby." See *The Book of Lies*, chapter 25.

The Stratagem and Other Stories. London: Mandrake Press, 1930.

The Sword of Song, Called by Christians the Book of the Beast. Benares: SPRT, 1904.

The Vision and the Voice with Commentary and Other Papers. Crowley, Aleister, Victor Neuburg and Mary Desti, ed. Hymenaeus Beta. York Beach, ME: Samuel Weiser, 1998.

The World's Tragedy. Foyers: SPRT, 1910. [2nd ed., Tempe, AZ: Falcon Press, 1985.]

Books by other authors

Achad, Frater. [Charles Stansfeld Jones]. *QBL or the Bride's Reception: Being a Short Cabalistic Treatise on the Nature and Use of the Tree of Life with a Brief Introduction and a Lengthy Appendix.* Chicago: Privately printed, 1922.

———. *Crystal Vision through Crystal Gazing or the Crystal as a Stepping-Stone to Clear Vision: A Practical Treatise on the Real Value of Crystal-Gazing.* Chicago: Yogi Publication Society, 1923.

———. *The Chalice of Ecstasy Being a Magical and Qabalistic Interpretation of the Drama of Parzival by a Companion of the Holy Grail.* Chicago: Yogi Publication Society, 1923.

———. *The Egyptian Revival or the Ever-Coming Son in Light of the Tarot.* Chicago: Collegium ad Spiritum Sanctum, 1923.

Amphlett Micklewright, F. H. "Aleister Crowley, Poet and Occultist." *The Occult Review* 1945, 72(2):41–6.

Anonymous. "Crowley's Safety Switch and Self-Acting Railway Signals." *The Mechanics' Magazine* 1853, 58(1537):66–7.

Arnold, Edwin. *The Light of Asia, or, The Great Renunciation (Mahhabhinishkramana): Being the Life and Teaching of Gautama, Prince of India and Founder of Buddhism.* London: Trübner, 1879.

Charles Barker & Sons. *The Joint Stock Companies' Directory for 1876.* London: John King & Co., 1867.

Codex Brucianus, MS Bruce 96, Bodleian Library, Oxford. [See also Mead, G. R. S., *Fragments of a Faith Forgotten: Some Short Sketches among the Gnostics, Mainly of the First Two Centuries. A Contribution to* the *Study of Christian Origins Based on the Most Recently Recovered Materials*, London: Theosophical Publishing Society, 1900.]

Dickens, Charles. "Self-Acting Railway Signals." *Household Words* 1853, 7(155, March 12):43–5.

———. "An Unsettled Neighborhood." *Household Words* 1854, 10(242, Nov. 11):289–92.

Eckartshausen, Karl von. *The Cloud Upon the Sanctuary*. Translated by Isabellede Steiger. Berwick, ME. Ibis Press, 2003.

Fuller, Jean Overton. *The Magical Dilemma of Victor Neuburg*. London: W. H. Allen, 1965.

Fuller, J.F.C. "Aleister Crowley 1898–1911: An Introductory Essay." In Keith Hogg, 666: *Bibliotheca Crowleyana: Catalogue of a Unique Collection of Books, Pamphlets, Proof Copies, MSS., etc., by, about, or connected with Aleister Crowley: Formed, and with an Introductory Essay, by Major-General J.F.C. Fuller*. Tenterden, Kent, 1966.

de Gebelin, Antoine Court. *Monde Primitif: Analysé et Comparé avec le Monde Moderne*. 9 vols. Paris: Chez Boudet, 1773–1782.

Glynn, Henry. *Reference Book to the Incorporated Railway Companies of England and Wales*. London: John Weale, 1847.

Goelet, Ogden. Raymond Oliver Faulkner, Eva Von Dassow, and James Wasserman. *The Egyptian Book of the Dead: The Book of Going Forth by Day: Being the Papyrus of Ani (Royal Scribe of the Divine Offerings)*. San Francisco: Chronicle Books, 1994, 1998.

Goetia. See Mathers, *Key of Solomon*; Crowley, *Book of the Goetia*.

Grant, Kenneth. *Remembering Aleister Crowley*. London: Skoob Books, 1991.

Gunther, J. Daniel. *Initiation in the Aeon of the Child: The Inward Journey*. Lake Worth, FL: Ibis Press, 2009.

Hall, Henry N. "Master Magician Reveals Weird Supernatural Rites." *The World Magazine*, 13 December 1914, pp. 9, 17.

Hamnett, Nina. *Laughing Torso*. London: Constable & Co., 1932.

Honourius, and Gösta Hedegård. *Liber Iuratus Honorii: A Critical Edition of the Latin Version of the Sworn Book of Honorius*. Acta Universitatis Stockholmiensis, 48. Stockholm, Sweden: Almqvist & Wiksell International, 2002.

Kaczynski, Richard. "Taboo and Transformation in the Works of Aleister Crowley." In Hyatt, Christopher (ed.), *Rebels and Devils*, 2nd ed. Tempe, AZ: New Falcon, 2000, pp. 171–9.

———. *Perdurabo: The Life of Aleister Crowley*. Tempe, AZ: New Falcon, 2002.

———. *Perdurabo Outtakes*. Blue Equinox Journal #1. Troy, MI: privately printed, 2005.

———. *Panic in Detroit: The Magician and the Motor City*. Blue Equinox Journal #2. Troy, MI: privately printed, 2005.

Kaplan, Aryeh. *Sefer Yetzirah: The Book of Creation*. York Beach, ME: Samuel Weiser, 1996.

Key of Solomon. See Mathers, *Key of Solomon*; and under Crowley, A Dead Hand.

Lee, A. H. E., & Nicholson, D. H. S. *The Oxford Book of English Mystical Verse*. Oxford: Clarendon Press, 1916.

Lévi, Éliphas. *Dogme et rituel de la haute magie*. Paris: G. Baillère, 1861. [*Dogma and Ritual of High Magic*.]

———. *La clef des grands mystères suivant Hénoch, Abraham, Hermés Trismégiste, et Salomon*. Paris: G. Baillière, 1861. [*The Key of the Mysteries*, translated from the French, with an introduction and notes by Aleister Crowley. *The Equinox* 1913, 1(10):supplement.]

Mannin, Ethel. *Confessions and Impressions*. London: Jarrolds, 1930.

Marchant, W. T. *In Praise of Ale; or, Songs, Ballads, Epigrams, & Anecdotes Relating to Beer, Malt, and Hops; with Some Curious Particulars Concerning Ale-wives and Brewers, Drinking-Clubs and Customs*. London: George Redway, 1888.

Mathers, Samuel Liddell. *The Key of Solomon the King (Clavicula Solomonis). Now First Translated and Edited from Ancient MSS in the British Museum*. London: Redway, 1889.

———. *The Book of the Sacred Magic of Abra-melin the Mage, as Delivered by Abraham the Jew unto His Son Lamech, A.D. 1458. Translated from the Original Hebrew into French, and Now Rendered from the Latter Language into English. From a Unique and Valuable MS in the 'Bibliotheque de l'Arsenal' at Paris*. London: J.M. Watkins, 1898.

———. *The Grimoire of Armadel*. York Beach, ME: Samuel Weiser, 1995.

Maugham, W. Somerset. *The Magician*. London: W. Heinemann, 1908.

Napoleon, Noel. *The History of the Brethren 1826–1936*. Edited by William Franklin Knapp. Denver, CO: W. F. Knapp, 1936.

Naylor, Anthony R. *Notes towards a Bibliography of Edward Crowley, together with Library Resources and Catalogue Information*. Thame: I-H-O Books, 2004.

Newton, Isaac. *The Principia: Mathematical Principles of Natural Philosophy*, 3rd ed, trans. I. Bernard Cohen and Anne Whitman. Berkeley: University of California Press, 1999 [1726].

Rabelais, François, and Terence Cave. *Gargantua and Pantagruel*. Everyman's Library (Series). London: David Campbell, 2001.

Rámanáthan, Ponnambalam. *The Gospel of Jesus according to St. Matthew, as Interpreted to B.L. Harrison by the Light of the Godly Experience of Sri Parananda*. London: Kegan Paul, Trench, Trübner Co., 1898.

———. *An Eastern Exposition of the Gospel of Jesus according to St. John, Being an Interpretation thereof by Sri Parananda by the Light of Jnana Yoga*. London: W. Hutchinson, 1902.

Rawson, Philip. *Sacred Tibet*. London, Thames and Hudson, 1991.

Spence, Richard B. "Secret Agent 666: Aleister Crowley and British Intelligence in America, 1914-1918." *International Journal of Intelligence and CounterIntelligence* 2000, 13(3):359–71.

———. *Secret Agent 666: Aleister Crowley, British Intelligence and the Occult.* Port Townsend, WA: Feral House, 2008.

Stephensen, P. R. *The Legend of Aleister Crowley, Being a Study of the Documentary Evidence Relating to a campaign of Personal Vilification Unparalleled in Literary History.* London: Mandrake Press, 1930. [Stephensen, P. R., & Crowley, Aleister. 2007. *The Legend of Aleister Crowley: A Study of the Facts.* Edited by Stephen J. King. Enmore: Helios Books.]

Tillyard, Aelfrida Catharine Wentenhall. *The Cambridge Poets 1900–1913.* Cambridge: W. Heffer, 1913.

Tuck, Henry. *Railway Directory for 1845: Containing the Names of the Directors and Principal Officers of the Railways in Great Britain.* London: Railway Times Office, 1845.

Urban, Hugh. *Magia Sexualis: Sex, Magic, and Liberation in Modern Western Esotericism.* Berkeley: University of California Press, 2006.

Wasserman, James. *The Mystery Traditions: Secret Symbols and Sacred Art.* Rochester, VT: Destiny Books, 2005.

———. and Nancy. *To Perfect This Feast: A Commentary on Liber XV, the Gnostic Mass.* West Palm Beach, FL: Sekmet Books, 2009.

Wasserman, Nancy. *The Weiser Concise Guide to Yoga for Magick.* San Francisco: Red Wheel/Weiser, 2007.

Wells, Colin. "Something Wicked This Way Comes." *Rock and Ice* 2004, 136 (September):58–61, 105–9.

Westcott, William Wynn. *The Pymander of Hermes.* London: Theosophical Society, 1894.

———. *The Chaldean Oracles of Zoroaster.* London: Theosophical Society, 1895.

Woodroffe, John. *The Garland of Letters: (Varnamâlâ) Studies in the Mantra-shâstra.* Madras: Ganesh, 1922.

Yates, Edmund Hodgson. *Edmund Yates: His Recollections and Experiences.* London: R. Bentley & Son, 1884.

ABOUT THE AUTHOR

RICHARD KACZYNSKI, PH.D., has been a student of the western mystery tradition—and of Thelema and the works of Aleister Crowley in particular—since 1977. He has been a member of O.T.O. since 1987, and an international lecturer on magick since 1990. He is the author of the critically-acclaimed biography *Perdurabo: The Life of Aleister Crowley*, as well as the books *Perdurabo Outtakes*, and *Panic in Detroit: The Magician and the Motor City*. Along with Hymenaeus Beta, he is co-editor of *The Revival of Magick and Other Essays*. Over the years, his writing has appeared in various magazines (*High Times, Different Worlds, The Magical Link, Mezlim, Eidolon, Neshamah, Cheth*) and in books (*Golden Dawn Sourcebook, Rebels and Devils*). He currently lives in Maryland with his wife and cat.

THE WEISER CONCISE GUIDES

A series, edited by James and Nancy Wasserman, designed to provide clear and accurate introductions to the most important disciplines of the Western Esoteric Tradition, each written by experts in the field. Broad overviews are augmented by explicit instructions for beginning and enhancing one's practice. Each author discusses the relevance of the subject to the personal life of the reader. Bibliographies of the best work in each field are included, allowing the reader to continue his or her studies with other authorities.

Alchemy—BRIAN COTNOIR
A guide to the theory and practice of alchemy with instructions on actually performing the alchemical work and setting up a laboratory for further experimentation. Illuminates both the spiritual and physical aspects of this ancient science and art.

Yoga for Magick—NANCY WASSERMAN
A guide to the theory and practice of yoga and meditation specifically designed for the practitioner of Western disciplines such as Magick, Wicca, Paganism, and Qabalah. Includes extensive information on diet and suggestions for pursuing a healthy lifestyle.

Herbal Magick—JUDITH HAWKINS-TILLIRSON
A guide to the theory and practice of herbalism, along with specific instruction in using herbs in magick. It provides a thorough overview of the relationship between herbalism, Qabalah, and astrology, along with a chapter on the magical system of Franz Bardon.

Practical Astrology—PRISCILLA COSTELLO
A guide to the theory and practice of astrology, including coherent summaries of planets, signs, houses, and aspects, to prepare the reader for an exciting demonstration of horoscope analysis. Includes numerous tables and charts and all astrological glyphs.

Check out:

www.redwheelweiser.com

or *www.studio31.com*

for future titles and more information on each book in this series.